RIPE FOR
DESSERT

RIPE FOR
DESSERT

David Lebovitz

100 Outstanding Desserts with Fruit—
Inside, Outside, Alongside

HarperCollins*Publishers*

ALSO BY David Lebovitz
Room for Dessert

FIRST EDITION

Designed by Vertigo Design, NYC

Photographs by Michael Lamotte

Art direction and prop styling by Sara Slavin

Food styling by David Lebovitz

Printed on acid-free paper

Library of Congress Cataloging-in-Publication Data

Lebovitz, David.

Ripe for dessert : 100 outstanding desserts with fruit—inside,
outside, alongside / David Lebovitz.—1st ed.

p.   cm.

ISBN 0-06-621246-4 (hardcover)

1. Desserts. 2. Cookery (Fruit). I. Title.

TX773 .L384   2003

641.8'6—dc21/2002032340

03 04 05 06 07 ❖/RRD 10 9 8 7 6 5 4 3 2 1

FOR FRED—
AND DESSERT LOVERS EVERYWHERE

x ACKNOWLEDGMENTS

xiii FOREWORD BY DEBORAH MADISON

xvi INTRODUCTION

17 APPLES, PEARS, QUINCE— AND RHUBARB!

18 Gravenstein Apple and Blackberry Crisp

20 Apple and Pear Crisp with Polenta Topping and Grappa-Soaked Raisins

21 Buckwheat Cake with Apples Poached in Cider

24 Apple Tart with Whole-Wheat Express Puff Pastry and Maple-Walnut Sauce

28 Spiced Apple Charlotte with Cider Sabayon

30 Apple and Quince Tarte Tatin

33 Quince Marmalade with Manchego Cheese

34 Stilton Shortcakes with Candied Pecans and Honey-Poached Pears

37 Marsala-Poached Pears Stuffed with Ricotta, Chocolate, Almonds, and Cherries

39 Frozen Caramel Mousse with Sherry-Glazed Pears, Chocolate, and Salted Almonds

42 Cornmeal Shortcakes with Spice-Baked Pears

44 Pear, Cherry, and Chocolate Bread Pudding

46 Polenta Cake with Saffron-Poached Pears

48 Rhubarb Tart with Almond Nougatine

51 TROPICAL FRUITS

53 Papaya Cake with Coconut Glaze

55 Kiwi, Pineapple, and Toasted Coconut Baked Hawaii

58 Mango Napoleons with Lime Custard and Coconut Flatties

63 Mango Tarte Tatin with Crushed Blackberries

65 Pineapple Coconut Cookies

66 Pineapple Frangipane Tart

69 Caramelized Pineapple Flan

71 Butterscotch Pudding with Coffee-Caramelized Bananas

74 Banana Cake with Mocha Icing and Coffee Crunchies

76 Mango and Lilikoi Butter

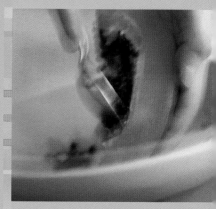

79 CITRUS FRUITS

81 Orange-Honey Fruit Salad with Bostock

83 Blood Orange Soup with Frozen Riesling Sabayon

84 Blood Orange Sorbet Surprise

86 Totally Orange Allspice Cake with Brown Sugar Glaze

88 Ricotta Cake with Candied Orange and Rosy Rhubarb Sauce

90 Anise-Orange Ice Cream Profiteroles with Chocolate Sauce

94 Buckwheat Crêpes with Tangerine Butterscotch Sauce

96 Jellied Tangerine Juice

97 Chocolate-Tangerine Sorbet

98 Lime Marshmallow Pie

101 Margarita Sorbet with Crispy Peanut Cookies

102 Lime Cream Puffs with Sugared Almonds and Coconut-Rum "Kaya"

104 Pink Grapefruit Champagne Sorbet

105 Free-Style Lemon Tartlets with White Chocolate Sauce

108 Lemon-Ginger Crème Brûlée

110 Lemon Quaresimali

112 Superlemon Soufflé

114 Quick-Candied Lemons

115 Gingery Lemonade

117 DRIED FRUITS

118 Chocolate Soufflé Cake with Prunes, Cranberries, and Kumquats in Port

121 Pear and Fig Chutney with Bittersweet Chocolate Mousse

122 Brazil Nut, Date, and Ginger Tart

124 Syrian-Style Date-Nut Torte

125 Date, Ginger, and Candied Pineapple Fruitcake

128 Prune, Coffee, Chocolate, and Amaretto Tiramisù

130 Prune Gâteau Basque

132 Chocolate Cherry Fruitcake

134 Absolute Best Brownies with Dried Cherries

136 Pistachio, Almond, and Cherry Bark

138 Peppery Chocolate-Cherry Biscotti

140 Apricot Ice Cream Tartufi

142 Apricot Filo Triangles with Retsina Syrup

145 Hazelnut, Apricot, and Chocolate Dacquoise with Apricot Sauce

147 Cranzac Cookies

149 FIGS, GRAPES, MELON, AND POMEGRANATES

150 Fresh Fig and Raspberry Tart with Honey

152 Homemade Ricotta with Fresh Figs and Chestnut Honey

153 Peanut, Butter, and Jelly Linzertorte

154 A Duo of Wine Grape Sorbets

155 Melon with Three Flavored Syrups

158 Watermelon and Sake Sorbet

159 Pomegranate Granita

161 STONE FRUITS

162 Cherry Sorbet for Dum-Dums with Almond Ding

164 Cherry Almond Cobbler

166 Chocolate Bread with Sautéed Cherries

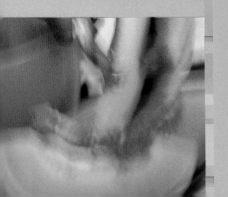

169 Chocolate and Fresh Candied Cherry Cake with Roasted Almond Crème Anglaise

171 Peaches in Red Wine

172 Peach and Amaretti Crisp

174 Peach Semifreddo

176 Peaches Poached in Wine Syrup

178 Apricot and Marzipan Tart

180 Nectarine and Blueberry Cobbler with Big Fluffy Biscuits

182 Nectarine and Raspberry Upside-Down Gingerbread

184 Spiced Plum Streusel Cake with Toffee Glaze

186 Plum, Nectarine, and Blackberry Charlotte

189 Three-Seed Shortcakes with Plums and Red Berries

191 Yeasted Plum Tart with Red Wine–Plum Sauce

193 BERRIES

194 Caramelized Brioche with Sugared Strawberries in Red Wine

197 Strawberries in Red Wine Syrup with Almond Meringue Baskets

199 Lindsey's Honeyed Strawberries al Formaggio

200 Strawberry Bavarian with Orange-Rhubarb Sauce

202 Berries Romanoff with Iced Sour Cream

203 Boysenberry Turnovers

207 Blackberry Financiers

208 Blackberry and Lemon Gratin

210 Ranch Panna Cotta with Blueberries

212 Mixed Berry Pie

214 Mascarpone Cheesecake with Mixed Berries

216 Mascarpone

217 Cassis Truffles

220 Tomato Jam with Rosemary Cookies

222 RECIPES BY TYPE

226 BIBLIOGRAPHY

228 INDEX

ACKNOWLEDGMENTS

I never dreamed I'd be writing my second cookbook, so sincere thanks to all of you who enjoyed baking from *Room for Dessert* and encouraged me to write another book.

Thanks to Fritz Streiff, who helped me say what I wanted to say, filling in my blanks as we hunched over our keyboards. I can't imagine what this book would be like without his help. Immense gratitude to my editor, Susan Friedland, for her support and friendship over the years; I'm lucky indeed to have such a terrific editor. Appreciation to editorial assistant Califia Suntree and production editor David Koral for being such pleasures to work with on the production of this book. And to the princess of publicity, Carrie Bachman: You're the best.

I am indebted to Sara Slavin and Michael Lamotte, for sharing and shaping my vision, for making the photographs as beautiful as they are, and for making the process so much fun yet again—even those two days at my house!

Thanks to seasoned photographer and budding chocolatier Greg Gorman, who found time to shoot me in between the real celebrities clamoring to get in front of his camera (and thanks to supermodel Joel West for helping with the dishes!).

Thanks to my agent, Fred Hill, who told me to just keep making desserts while he took care of all the details, which he does wonderfully.

My appreciation to Shari Saunders for helping me in the kitchen with some of the recipe testing, development, and the piles of dishes. I am so grateful to all the members of my baking family who generously provide advice, knowledge, and, sometimes, recipes: Tim Armitage, Anne Block, Kelley Heldt, Rochelle Huppin-Fleck, Emily Luchetti (who provided great advice on my first endeavor), Manï Niall, Helene Siegel, John Scharffenberger, Robert Steinberg, Mary Jo Thoresen, and Dede Wilson—with extra special gratitude to Flo Braker and Nick Malgieri for answering my endless questions about baking and cookbook writing.

I owe much of what I know about baking to Lindsey Shere, who will always, unassumingly, be my teacher and mentor, and to the influence of Alice Waters, with her passion for food that's good and simple. My gratitude to both Lindsey and Alice for planting the seed that grew.

Thanks to Susan Feniger and Mary Sue Milliken of Border Grill and Ciudad restaurants for lending me their lively glasses and dinnerware. And to Chris Hubbuch and Brian Maynard at KitchenAid for their continued support—and for keeping me clean.

And thanks to my recipe testers, ace bakers on their own: Clifford Colvin, Rob Gallagher, Bunny Gottlieb, Veronica Segredo, and Fritz Streiff.

FOREWORD by Deborah Madison

Fruit is the most seductive of foods. Its allure begins with the promise of its blossoms. There are the honey-scented masses of almond flowers in February, the simple little strawberry flowers in June, the outrageously complex flowers of the passion fruit. Then comes the fruit itself, with its shadings of subtle or outrageous hues, surface features such as the dappling of sugar spots on a nectarine, the fuzzy coating of a quince, a blush of pink on a golden delicious apple. There's the inky blackness of blackberries, the molten orange translucence of a dead ripe persimmon, the beads of syrup forming on the surface of a ripe fig, the frosty bloom on a plum. There is no end to the beauty of fruit, so it's no wonder that David Lebovitz begins *Ripe for Dessert* by declaring that fruit is his passion. While my passion has long been vegetables, I have to admit that fruit goes beyond vegetables in the realm of seductiveness, because it has a lot of what vegetables don't always have, and that's perfume.

I've noticed that when people buy fruit at the supermarket, they pick a plum, a handful of cherries, a pear, and then put it right into their plastic bags. What's missing is that hopeful gesture that raises a fruit, stem end forward, towards the nose for that deep inhalation meant to detect scent and its promise of flavor. The test of its worth. Without flavor and perfume, the world of fruit falls flat, rests on looks alone, and turns blandly one dimensional. The perfume is really more important than the looks, as beguiling as they may be, for it points us to flavor—and that's what matters most, after all. In general, it works this way, but not always, for some fruits hold the keys to their flavor close. Take the passion fruit, which doesn't so much as hint at the sexy tropical scents that lie concealed beneath its dry, purple husk. But most other fruits let their secrets fly, like a white peach, which tells you all you need to know with one inhalation.

Fortunately, David is not only passionate about fruit, but also very helpful about untangling some of its mysteries as he courses through his recipes with hints of what to look for, what to expect, what to avoid.

We've heard a lot about cooking and eating seasonally with vegetables, but I think that seasonal eating is even more important when it comes to fruit—that is, if you want real excitement and satisfaction. Unless you make an effort to look closer to the source for the kind of fruit David is talking about, the actual attainment of good fruit can be a challenge. Sourcing is always the key to success in the kitchen, whether it's fruit or vegetables you're looking for, or it's your kitchen or a restaurant's. Fruit that gives so much flavor that overlays of sugar and butter and cream aren't even necessary (then imagine the overlays!) is what makes these recipes so vibrant, not fussy technique. But where do we find such fruit? You can follow David's example with trips to the farmers' market, delving into the blackberry vines at a U-pick, or driving to the country for the new apples coming on at an antique apple orchard. Fruit that can be found at its source is going to have the most promise for us in the kitchen. Of course, this means that it's going to be, most often, local and seasonal, so we end up moving through a year of fruits and desserts in a happily predictable way. It's not surprising that David says he goes a little loony when cherry season finally begins, and why not? He's certainly not cooking with fresh cherries in December. He's a seasonal cook and all seasonal cooks that I know go loony when a favorite fruit or vegetable finally comes around.

Bring any of David's desserts forward at the close of a meal and you'll have a hard time remaining humble under showers of praise. But what I especially like about David's book, aside from the results his recipes promise, is David himself—that he and his desserts are so approachable, relaxed, and friendly. You don't have to hold your breath to make them, and you can make a cake just because it makes you, or someone else, feel better. What better reason to make dessert? They're fun to make and a pleasure to eat. Although I saw David working away in the Chez Panisse kitchen for many years, these desserts feel like they come from home. The home of an exceptionally fine pastry chef, but his home nonetheless. Here's a person who just loves to bake and is having a great time doing it! Such enthusiasm is delightfully infectious, assuring that we'll have a great time making David's desserts, too.

RIPE FOR
DESSERT

INTRODUCTION

Welcome to my second book!
It seems like a long time since I've
been in print, but the response to my
first book was so terrific that I knew
I had to wait until I came up with the
right idea for this one. After a wise
friend said to me, "You need to follow
your passion," I followed his advice.

My passion is fruit: buying a fragrant peach or a pear that is still slightly firm, but with the promise of a fantastic sweet aroma . . . or a basket of blackberries, so delicate, with an inklike sheen (I generally eat most of them on the way home). I know it sounds funny, but I just love the heft of a plump Comice pear, or a sweet-heavy crimson nectarine. And, to me, there's nothing more satisfying than spitting the pit from a perfectly plump Bing cherry or cradling a sweet, velvety peach in my hand, holding it ever so gently, anticipating the promise of sweet, slippery slices. Whenever I go to the farmer's market I invariably buy way too much fruit and have to lug my overstuffed canvas satchel back home where I lay out everything I've bought. I must say, I treat pieces of fruit and baskets of berries like tender, delicate children that need to be nurtured until they mature to ripe perfection.

Working in restaurants year after year exposed me to many different kinds of fruit. My years at Chez Panisse were especially fulfilling because our vendors consistently offered the finest—and sometimes the most unusual—fruits available. As baker at a Southeast Asian restaurant I learned about exotic and unusual tropical fruits, which my co-workers revered and were always eager to explain to me and have me taste. I was astounded by the intense and unusual fruity (and sometimes not so fruity) flavors that I sampled. Living in California, I am fortunate to have many wonderful fruits available locally. Traveling across the country, I've marveled at gorgeous berries in the Midwest, enjoyed crisp apples in Washington, picked jewel-like red currants in New York, and slurped juicy mangoes and papaya on the beaches in Hawaii.

This is a book of recipes in which these beautiful fruits lift dessert to new levels. For example, polenta cake is terrific on its own, but when accompanied by saffron-poached pears it's elevated from a humble cake into a sumptuous sensation. Other fruit compotes, sauces, and garnishes enhance other dishes—coffee-caramelized bananas brighten butterscotch pudding, warm cherries lap at chocolate bread, strawberries in red wine are soaked up by brioche—and I've tried to include plenty of suggestions for other, similarly enlivening combinations. But I'll be happiest if readers of this book use their imaginations and start to make connections on their own. Why not thumb through the book, and get so curious about, say, berries macerated in a touch of sweet balsamic vinegar that you'll have to do some inventing on your own without further guidance? What about *other* fruits macerated in balsamic?

For those of you who are looking for healthier ways to live, eating fresh fruit desserts with a minimum of butter and cream is certainly a place to begin. I've come to crave the intense flavors of fresh fruit-juice reductions and now I make ice creams and sauces with less cream and butter, but infinitely more flavor. In many ice cream and custard recipes I've reduced the traditional quantities of heavy cream, replacing it with half-and-half or even milk. The customary abundance of butter in desserts has been trimmed just a tad to allow fruit flavors to shine as much as possible and whole eggs sometimes replace egg yolks. But one thing I never ever skimp on is flavor. This is not a book of austere desserts.

Among the luscious recipes you'll find great rich chocolate cakes (I love chocolate), warm fruit cobblers, and tangy lime pies. Many of these desserts can be made well before you want to serve them, too. Most fruit compotes, for example, profit from steeping in their flavorful liquid. (Also, fruits that may be less than perfect often benefit from being warmed with spices or other flavors.)

Why do I bake? People often ask me that question, and the real answer never occurred to me until I read a passage in Nick Malgieri's book *How to Bake.* Nick quoted a fellow baker saying, "Bake something, you'll feel better!" Yes, I admit it, I really love to get in the kitchen and bake something up. It does make me feel better. And to share the results with friends afterward is really the icing on the cake, so to speak!

But that doesn't mean I want to spend all day in the kitchen, nor do I suspect you do, either. And sometimes I can't find the time to do too much running around in search of unusual ingredients (although I live in a city and it can be great fun). No recipe in this book requires any tool more esoteric than a candy thermometer, which is sold in most super-markets. And all the ingredients in the recipes were gathered at either my local grocery store or the produce market.

I love to get my hands in things—slicing vibrant tangerines and squeezing them until the juice runs out. I love to slip on my old, tattered red shirt for the messy task of pitting ripe Bing cherries (a white T-shirt would end up looking like a Jackson Pollock painting), or chatting with some friends in the kitchen as we take on the task of peeling a basket of crisp fall apples to make an apple crisp for dinner guests.

I hope that through this book you discover the fun of baking and share the pleasure that I get from creating recipes you and your friends will enjoy and want to make over and over.

THINGS YOU SHOULD KNOW BEFORE YOU BAKE

Bittersweet and bitter chocolate are not the same thing. Bitter chocolate has no sugar. Bittersweet chocolate has sugar and cocoa butter to make it smooth. Bittersweet chocolate and semisweet chocolate are interchangeable in all my recipes but avoid using chips for melting as some brands may be difficult to melt smoothly.

Chocolate and small amounts of water aren't a good mix. When melting chocolate by itself, the tiniest amount of water can cause chocolate to seize and harden. Wipe bowls and utensils clean and dry before melting any chocolate.

Cocoa powder is always unsweetened. Neither hot cocoa mix nor powdered chocolate are the same thing as cocoa powder: Both contain sweeteners, and sometimes other ingredients.

Check your thermometer. Get a scale. If you're unsure if your candy thermometer is correct, boil some water; at sea level, the thermometer should read 212 degrees F. Get a scale. You don't need one that is the pinnacle of scientific accuracy, but a digital baking scale will make weighing chocolate and other ingredients much simpler and more accurate.

Use the right kinds of measuring cups. For liquids, a see-through measuring cup works best. Set the cup on a level surface for an accurate reading. Graduated measuring cups (the kind that stack inside each other, with handles) are the only ones to use for dry ingredients such as flour, sugar, and cocoa powder.

Measure flour correctly. Store it in a wide canister so it's easy to spoon the flour into a graduated measuring cup, and then level it with the straight edge of a knife. Don't pack it in or tamp it down.

Read a recipe all the way through before beginning. No one is more impatient than I am to eat, so I've kept my recipes reasonably short. But you don't want to get halfway through a recipe and realize that you need something at room temperature.

Gather all your ingredients first and set them all out before you assemble anything. Professionals call this the *mise en place,* which means "placed in position." This way you won't put your cake in the oven and then turn around to realize that you've forgotten to add the eggs. (Of course, I've never done this, I've just heard of others who have . . .)

When whipping egg whites, a small amount of fat can be a problem. Make sure your bowl and whisk are free of any traces of egg yolks or butter, which can cause your whites not to whip properly. Stray bits of egg yolk can easily be removed from the whites by using the jagged edge of an eggshell. And don't beat egg whites in plastic bowls, because they retain a certain amount of oily residue despite your best cleaning efforts.

Use heavy-duty, heavy-gauge cookware. Sturdy cookware will last a long time—the best brands have lifetime guarantees—and will resist burning and warping. It will be a pleasure to use. Flimsy cookware isn't worth the money.

When directed to grease a pan for baking, I prefer to use butter. A thin layer is usually all that's necessary. The wrappers folded around sticks of butter work well for greasing pans. When a recipe calls for a pan to be lined with parchment paper, greasing the pan is often unnecessary, unless specifically called for.

Use best-quality ingredients. Spend the small amount of extra money on great-tasting chocolate, plump dried fruits, and the most fragrant fruits and berries you can find. It's become a cliché to preach to people to shop for produce only when it is in season, but it's really true that that's when it's most abundant and at its best, and at the most reasonable price, and that's the time to use it.

I use coarse salt when baking. Coarse kosher and sea salts are less harsh than table salt. While you usually use such a small amount in baking, it's not an issue. In certain recipes, like the Crispy Peanut Cookies (page 101), however, it becomes important.

Wash fruits before using them. You should rinse fruits and towel dry them before eating, unless you're discarding the skin. I don't wash berries, except strawberries and blueberries, because I think it destroys some of their delicate aroma, but if you feel you must, spread them on a towel to dry before using.

"Can this be frozen?" When I teach cooking classes, invariably hands shoot up as I am finishing a dessert, and I am asked this question. Finally, at one class I asked why everyone was so eager to freeze all these beautiful, freshly made desserts? (Besides, who has room in their freezer? Mine's so packed you couldn't wedge a dime in there.) I was told that things need to be frozen if you're entertaining. And here I always thought that when you entertained you were supposed to knock yourself out completely until your guests arrive, then collapse in a heap when they leave. Fortunately, not everyone entertains as I do, so whenever something *can* be made in advance and refrigerated or frozen without any sacrifice in quality, it's noted in the recipe. (Note to self: Change the way you entertain.)

Follow your instincts. Alas, I can't be in your kitchen with you when you're baking, which is unfortunate because all ovens are different, pans differ slightly in size, and even measuring spoons and cups aren't precisely the same. So if something looks done, even though the recipe may say it needs more time, take it out of the oven. Or if the berries you brought home taste as if they need an extra sprinkle of sugar, they're probably slightly more tart than the ones I used, and you should go right ahead and add a little sugar.

Above all, have fun! Although now I bake at home a great deal, I was lucky enough to bake professionally for many years, and I know that baking can be both a meditative activity and something that's wildly fun. Some folks like to take on big baking projects while others want to make something simple that's delicious to eat. Either way, enjoy the whole process from shopping for the ingredients to mixing up a creamy batter to serving something you made yourself to friends and family.

WHAT THE HECK DOES DAVID MEAN?

Here are my definitions of some of the words and phrases that you will come across in this book.

Beat: Beating means stirring firmly with a spoon or spatula to mix together. With an electric mixer, this is done best with the flat paddle or beater.

Boil: To cook over medium to high heat. A boiling mixture bubbles vigorously and moves about.

Chop: To chop finely means using a chef's knife (or a food processor) to cut the ingredient(s) into little pieces about the size of BBs. To chop coarsely means to cut something into pieces about the size of a small pea.

Cream: To cream means to beat butter together with sugar or other ingredients until smooth and (sometimes) fluffy.

Fold: Folding is a lifting action, almost always done with a flexible rubber spatula, which gently combines ingredients or mixtures that are airy and subject to deflation. Folding is best done by scraping the spatula in a stroke against the side of the bowl and, at the end of the stroke, lifting the spatula and moving the mixture toward the center. Lighter ingredients and mixtures are always folded into heavier ones.

Nonreactive: Refers to metal that won't react when in contact with something acidic, such as wine and/or fruit juices. Nickel-lined copper, stainless steel, anodized aluminum, and nonstick surfaces are all nonreactive. Knives, strainers, and other cookware that are not made of stainless steel should not be used for fruit.

Pulverize: When referring to nuts, this means to process them in a food processor until ground up into a fine powder with the consistency of coarse cornmeal or ground coffee. Processing nuts with sugar or flour helps keep the ground nuts powdery, not pasty. Pulverizing toasted nuts that are still warm should be avoided; warm nuts release too much oil.

Reduce: To reduce means to remove excess liquid and is best done over low to medium heat, at a simmer. Reduction intensifies flavors and thickens liquids so there is less need to add thickeners or fats.

Room temperature: Ingredients at room temperature are between 60 and 70 degrees F. Eggs and butter should reach room temperature if they are removed from the refrigerator 30 to 45 minutes before you need to use them. Eggs separate more easily when cold. Once out of their shells, however, they should be used right away. Therefore, separate them at room temperature, right before you need them. Cold eggs in the shell can be brought to room temperature by submerging them in very warm water for about 5 minutes. Butter will reach room temperature faster if it's cut into 1/2-inch pieces.

Saucepan: For the recipes in this book, a small saucepan holds about 2 quarts; a medium-size saucepan, between 4 and 6 quarts; and a large saucepan is one that holds more than 6 quarts.

Simmer: To cook over low heat. Something is simmering when steam rises from it and tiny bubbles very gently break the surface.

Skillet: A medium-size skillet is a heavy frying pan between 6 and 8 inches in diameter; a large skillet has a diameter greater than 8 inches.

Stir: Stirring "constantly" means that you must stand over whatever you're stirring and stir without stopping. Stirring "frequently" means stirring every so often, usually every 20 to 30 seconds. Use a wooden spoon or heatproof utensil.

Toast: Nuts are toasted to enhance their flavor and aroma. Most whole nuts should be toasted in a single layer on a baking sheet in a 350 degree F oven for 8 to 10 minutes, stirring once or twice, until colored light brown throughout. Cool before using.

Whip: Whip means to use a wire whisk (see next), not just to combine but to incorporate air, increasing volume and lightening a mixture, as when you whip cream. Unlike stirring, whipping is a vigorous circular lifting motion that literally lifts the mixture from the bowl. If you have an electric mixer, use the whisk attachment.

Whisk: I use "whisk together" to mean "combine ingredients thoroughly with a whisk." A whisk is also used for beating egg mixtures to eliminate lumps and for stirring dry ingredients together when sifting is not necessary.

SELECTING AND STORING FRUIT

The following is a guide to the proper selection and storage of the fruits in this book. Because all these desserts depend on fruit for flavor, it's wise to seek out and use the very best fruit you can find. Besides farmers' markets and farm stands, smaller produce stores are often the best places to buy fruit, since the grocer may seek out varieties supermarkets do not carry.

Apples: Apples are best in the fall and winter. The rest of the year they have been held in cold storage and can be mealy and not at their best. Select apples with no bruises. Good apples often have an appealing aroma, and their skins will be smooth and unwrinkled, indicating that the flesh is moist and juicy. I always peel apples (and remove their cores and seeds) before cooking them, because the peels don't soften much during baking. Store apples in the refrigerator or in a cool place until ready to use.

Apricots: Their brief summer season means making the most of fresh apricots when you see them at the market. My favorite variety is the Royal Blenheim. Apricots are usually sold still firm and need further ripening at room temperature. Any with green on the skins were picked too soon; so don't buy them. A nice blush, on the other hand, indicates that they were basking in the sun before they were picked. Store apricots so as not to bruise them while they ripen; I set them carefully on a towel. They are fully ripe, succulent, and utterly sweet when squishy and translucent. When ripe, refrigerate them and use quickly as they will continue to soften. Baking accentuates apricots' tartness, and they will need more sugar than you think, so don't be tempted to use less sugar than the recipes call for.

Bananas: Most commercial bananas are sold unripe and firm, sometimes still tinged with green. Let them ripen at room temperature. Ripe bananas should be used right away and refrigerated unpeeled only if they will be cooked later. Cold, their flesh turns dense and oily. The flesh of other banana varieties, including yellow burros and red bananas, must be quite soft before it is fully ripe (the skin of red bananas will have turned close to black). Puréed bananas can be stored in the refrigerator for up to 5 days (the surface will brown slightly, which is fine) or frozen for several months. Unpeeled whole ripe bananas can also be frozen. They should sit at room temperature to thaw at least 20 minutes before being peeled and used only for cooking.

Blackberries, Blueberries, and Raspberries: Perhaps the most fragile and delicate fruits available, berries are laborious to pick, so use them wisely. Check the bottom of the baskets; excessive wetness can mean they are more likely to be going bad. Purchase raspberries, blackberries, and blueberries only in the summer, when they are in season. Do not encourage importers to tease us with flavorless berries in the winter! Blueberries are sturdier, but all other berries should be used within a day, or refrigerated and used within 2 days. I don't rinse raspberries or blackberries before using them, as it seems to result in a loss of delicacy. If you do, gently pat them dry afterward. Raspberries, blackberries, and blueberries can all be frozen successfully: Spread them in an even layer on a baking sheet or platter and put it in the freezer. Once the berries are frozen hard, transfer them to freezer bags, seal, and freeze for up to 6 months. Fresh berries that are not prefrozen before bagging will freeze into a solid mass when bagged and are difficult to separate and thaw. Frozen berries are best cooked or puréed into a sauce or sorbet or added, still frozen, to a pie, crisp, or cobbler filling.

Cherries: The short cherry season lasts about a month or so, beginning with much excitement in mid May. Choose cherry varieties you like. The best are red Bings (said to have been named after a Chinese gardener), Vans, and Tartarians. Yellow varieties have a more delicate flavor and are pretty mixed with red ones. Fresh sour cherries are unfortunately harder to come by, but they are really delicious when baked. Choose plump, unblemished cherries. Moist stems mean the cherries were picked recently. Cherries are picked ripe and should be stored in the refrigerator and eaten within a day or two for best flavor. To preserve cherries, make the compote of warm cherries on page 167 and keep it in the refrigerator for up to a week, or freeze it, well sealed, for up to 6 months. Uncooked pitted cherries can be frozen the same way the compote can.

Citrus Fruits: The best citrus fruit is harvested in the wintertime. This is especially true of Ruby grapefruit, Navel oranges, Meyer lemons, and blood oranges, as well as most tangerines. Buy all citrus fruits the same way: Select fruits that are heavy for their size with no soft spots or bruises. If you are going to use the zest, it is prudent to use organic or unsprayed citrus. Otherwise, wash and dry the fruit before zesting. Citrus fruits yield more juice at room temperature when squeezed than cold citrus because the juice cells inside are soft and break open easily. Rolling the fruit firmly on the counter helps rupture these cells, increasing the yield of juice. Store all citrus fruit in the refrigerator. Citrus juice can be frozen successfully, but avoid refrigerating it for longer than 8 hours or it will taste bitter.

Dried Fruit: The choicest dried fruits of any kind are plump and moist. Some people prefer unsulphured dried fruit, although it is often less attractive than sulphured fruit because sulphur prevents discoloration. That said, you can use them interchangeably. Check to see if the dried fruit you're about to buy has added sugar (most don't, which is best). I use only California dried apricots, which are tart and tangy; most imported varieties are bland and flavorless. Prunes were recently given a name change by their industry marketing board and are now supposed to be referred to only as "dried plums." That is exactly what they are, of course, but many bakers still refer to them as prunes, and they are now labeled both ways.

Kiwi Fruit: Almost all kiwi fruit is grown in New Zealand or California, where it was heavily planted after it became the signature fruit of nouvelle cuisine. Kiwi fruit should be quite soft when used. If they are to be puréed, the softer the better. Hard, unripe kiwi can be ripened at room temperature, although if they were picked too soon, they will soften but remain acidic within. The skin is edible, but rather unpleasant. I recommend that you peel it away; use a sharp knife.

Mangoes: Mangoes ripen in the spring and summer. Look for mangoes that feel heavy and smell sweet. Hayden and Tommy Atkins are good varieties that are widely grown in Mexico. In the market they should look colorful and plump, in vivid reds and yellows with perhaps slight traces of green. Haitian mangoes can also be excellent: only the bright yellow-orange ones should be used for baking. Green mangoes will not ripen; they are meant to be eaten that way in salads. Ripe mangoes should be used right away or refrigerated for a day or two at the most. Any longer and they will begin to taste tired. Peel away the skin with a sharp knife. Cut the flesh away from the pit and remove any inedibly fibrous flesh surrounding it, getting as close as possible. Mango slices can be sealed in freezer bags and frozen for up to 6 months.

Papayas: Latin and Asian markets often have the best selection of papayas. I like to buy the large Mexican papayas, which have brilliant red flesh and lots of spicy seeds and are usually very ripe. The seeds are edible and are said to aid digestion. Like Mexican papayas, the small papayas from Hawaii, both yellow- and red-fleshed, are ripe when slightly soft. Firm papayas will ripen at room temperature; once soft they should be refrigerated or used right away.

Passion Fruit or Lilikoi: The ultimate tropical treat, this ethereal fruit can be hard to find at grocers and supermarkets, even though it is obtainable all year long from specialty produce importers. The passion fruit vine can be very prolific; in climates warm enough for it, you often find its fruit piled up at small markets and fruit stands. Choose passion fruit that are slightly soft, even wrinkled. Split the fruit in half and scrape seeds and pulp into a nonreactive strainer. Press down to strain out the seeds from the pulpy juice, which loses none of its sweet-tart flavor and aroma when frozen. (The seeds are edible, too, if you like them, which I do.) Some Latin markets sell frozen passion fruit purée. It can also be purchased from bakery suppliers.

Peaches and Nectarines: Nothing symbolizes summer for me the way peaches and nectarines do. The most delicious peaches and nectarines are picked just before they reach full ripeness, so your best bet is to shop at a farmer's market or a farm stand, where the peaches for sale have been allowed to ripen the longest on the tree. Look for unbruised fruit, with no green on the skin. At home, ripen peaches and nectarines by setting them stem end down on a towel, to prevent bruising, at room temperature. When they are slightly soft and sweet-smelling, use them right away. You can refrigerate them for up to 2 days, but by doing that they lose some of the sweet fragrance that makes them so special.

Pears: Unlike most other fruits, pears need to be picked unripe and ripened off the tree. Some varieties, such as Comice and Seckel, have an irresistible heady fragrance when eaten raw. The fragrance and flavors of other varieties, such as Bosc pears, come forward best when they are cooked. Pears should be stored upright and freestanding to prevent bruising and ripened at room temperature until slightly soft to the touch midway up the stem end. Once they are ripe, refrigerate them until ready to use. (Pears ripen deceptively, from the center outward, so make sure that the ones you buy are not already overripe, as can often be the case toward the end of pear season, in midwinter.) I always peel pears for cooking and remove the core and seeds as well as the fibrous strings that run from the stem end to the base.

Pineapple: Almost all the pineapples we consume are from Mexico and Hawaii, harvested and brought to market all year. Once picked, they do little, if any, further ripening. So choose one that is labeled Jet-Fresh or Field-Fresh, which indicates that the pineapple was cut ripe from the plant. A perfect pineapple should have skin that is yellow, not green. The fruit should yield slightly to pressure, and, above all, smell intensely of sweet tropical pineapple. To prepare, twist off the leafy top with your hands, and peel down the sides with a sharp knife. Remove the eyes with a nonreactive vegetable peeler, quarter the pineapple lengthwise, then cut away the firm core on each of the pieces. Pineapple pieces can be frozen in freezer bags for up to 6 months and used for baking.

Plums: Plums vary from puckery wild varieties the size of olives to jumbo hybrids such as the supersweet yellow Shinko. Baking plums marries the flavor from their tart skins and sweet flesh. Choose firm, plump ones; plums are ready to eat when slightly soft. Keep them on the counter until fully ripe, then refrigerate until ready to use. A pluot is a cross between an apricot and a plum and is a fine substitute for plums in any recipe. Pluots ripen similarly to plums.

Quince: Whether ripe or unripe, a quince should be rock-hard. The skin of a ripe quince will have turned from green to a pale yellow, and most quince will give off an unbelievable aroma that can fill a room quite dramatically. Wipe away any fuzz on the outside with a dishcloth, quarter the quince, then carefully peel away the flesh and cut out the core. Be careful! The firm flesh can resist being cut. Store quince at room temperature until ripe, then refrigerate.

Rhubarb: Although hothouse rhubarb is available year-round, brilliant red, field-grown rhubarb is mostly a late-winter to spring crop. Rhubarb should be refrigerated until you're ready to cook it. Then rinse it thoroughly to remove any dirt, trim away any leaves, and slice the stems. Sliced rhubarb can be bagged in freezer bags and frozen for up to 6 months.

Strawberries: You may see strawberries in the market all year long, but watch out. Most of the year they are tart with little flavor. And they'll be expensive. Good strawberries appear in the spring, depending on the climate, and steadily improve in flavor and sweetness as the weather becomes warmer and drier. Look for deep red berries with few bruises (some of the best varieties are very fragile and may have soft spots). Don't buy moldy berries. Any hint of white or green near the stem indicates that the strawberry is underripe. So does a "cat's nose," the cluster of seeds at the pointy end. Strawberries should be spread out on a plate in one layer to prevent crushing and bruising, and lightly rinsed before using to remove any grit. It's fine to leave them out on the counter if you plan to use them within a day. Otherwise they should be refrigerated. Whole strawberries that have been hulled and strawberry purée can be frozen, for up to 6 months, but defrosted berries should not be substituted for fresh, except in a sauce or sorbet, or baked in a pie, crisp, or cobbler.

Where I live, these are the fruits of autumn, winter, and the early spring: crisp apples, lush pears, fragrant quince, tangy rhubarb. I love them all, whether baked into a crisp, simply poached, or caramelized in a classic tart. Do they seem ill-matched? Rhubarb isn't even a fruit, after all, it's the stalks of a succulent perennial; and apples, pears, and quinces are all harvested in the late summer and fall, months before garden rhubarb starts poking up. But pears and apples keep me going throughout the winter, and to me, with rhubarb, they are the quintessential fresh fruits of the long coastal rainy season, when fresh bush-berries and stone fruits are months away.

APPLES, PEARS, QUINCE —AND RHUBARB!

GRAVENSTEIN APPLE AND BLACKBERRY CRISP

8 SERVINGS

THE TOPPING:

¾ cup flour

1¼ cups walnuts or pecans, finely chopped

¼ cup granulated sugar

½ cup firmly packed light brown sugar

½ teaspoon ground cinnamon

½ teaspoon salt

8 tablespoons (1 stick) unsalted butter, cut into 1-inch cubes and chilled

THE FILLING:

10 to 12 Gravenstein apples or other good baking apples (about 3½ pounds)

¼ cup granulated sugar

1½ cups blackberries

1½ teaspoons vanilla extract

I always get a tad melancholy in August when the first crop of Gravenstein apples comes into the markets. Call it Seasonal Apple Disorder. To me, the beginning of apple season means the impending finale of all the summer fruits, from plentiful berries to luscious, ripe peaches and plums.

My cure is to take a drive to The Apple Farm in the Anderson Valley, north of San Francisco, owned and operated by Sally and Bob Schmitt and their daughter Karen. As I drive up there, the roadside blackberry bushes along the way are still bearing juicy fruit, and I stop and pick a few, mindful of the rattlesnakes that share my affection for these blackberry bushes. The farm itself is a bucolic orchard of many apple varieties, some of them rare heirlooms; all of them exceptional, like the Gravenstein. A visit is enough to remind me that fall and winter fruits like apples and pears are just as precious as summertime stone fruits such as cherries and apricots. And as long as their harvest overlaps with the last of the ripening berries, we can enjoy desserts like this irresistible berry and apple crisp.

It may look as if this recipe calls for too much fruit and makes too much topping, but the apples cook down substantially and I like a lot of topping. So really pack in the apples and pile up the topping.

I **To make the topping:** Stir together the flour, nuts, sugars, cinnamon, and salt. Add the butter and mix it into the flour mixture with a pastry blender or electric mixer until the butter is broken up into small pieces, working it until the topping is just beginning to clump together and looks crumbly rather than sandy.

2   **To make the filling:** Peel and quarter the apples. Remove the cores and cut the apples into $\frac{1}{4}$- to $\frac{1}{2}$-inch slices. Mix together the apple slices with the granulated sugar, blackberries, and vanilla.

3   To bake the crisp, position one oven rack in the center of the oven and another below it in the lower third. Place a sheet of aluminum foil on the lower rack to catch any fruit juices that bubble over. Preheat the oven to 350 degrees.

4   Pack the apple mixture firmly into a shallow 2-quart baking dish. Distribute the topping over the apple mixture, being sure to get plenty of topping in the corners (so no one gets shortchanged).

5   Bake the crisp for 1 hour, until the top is deep golden brown and a knife can be easily inserted into the center, indicating the apples are soft and fully cooked.

Variations: For apple and cranberry crisp, substitute 1 cup of fresh or frozen cranberries for the blackberries.

For apple and mince crisp, make an "express" mincemeat by mixing together 1 apple or pear, peeled, cored, and grated; $\frac{1}{3}$ cup orange marmalade; $\frac{1}{4}$ cup raisins; 2 tablespoons brown sugar; 2 tablespoons brandy; $\frac{1}{2}$ teaspoon vanilla extract; $\frac{1}{2}$ teaspoon ground cinnamon; and $\frac{1}{4}$ teaspoon ground cloves. (Although you can use this mincemeat right away, to "cure" it a bit, store it in the refrigerator for up to a week, stirring once or twice.) When ready to make the crisp, mix the mincemeat with 10 to 12 apples, prepared as for the recipe above, omitting the sugar and blackberries.

APPLE AND PEAR CRISP WITH POLENTA TOPPING AND GRAPPA-SOAKED RAISINS

8 SERVINGS

THE FRUIT FILLING:

¾ cup raisins

3 tablespoons grappa

6 apples (about 2 pounds)

6 pears (about 2 pounds)

⅓ cup granulated sugar

1½ teaspoons vanilla extract

THE TOPPING:

¾ cup flour

⅔ cup polenta or stone-ground cornmeal

½ cup walnuts, almonds, or pecans, toasted

½ cup firmly packed light brown sugar

1 teaspoon ground cinnamon

8 tablespoons (1 stick) butter, salted or unsalted, cut into ½-inch pieces and chilled

Note: The polenta topping can be made ahead, sealed in a plastic bag, and refrigerated for up to 1 week or frozen for up to 6 months.

Crisps need plenty of fruit mounded up in the baking dish when they go into the oven because as fruit bakes it releases moisture and cooks down, intensifying the flavor. This particular topping uses almost as much cornmeal as flour, which gives this winter fruit crisp an appealing crunchiness.

1 **To make the fruit filling:** Toss the raisins with the grappa in a large bowl and let stand for 30 to 60 minutes, until most of the grappa has been absorbed. Peel and core the apples and the pears. Cut them into ⅓-inch slices, and toss them together in the bowl with the grappa-soaked raisins, the sugar, and vanilla. Pack the fruit mixture into a 2-quart baking dish. It may seem like a lot, but it will cook down considerably.

2 Position one oven rack in the center of the oven and another below it in the lower third. Place a sheet of aluminum foil on the lower rack to catch any fruit juices that bubble over. Preheat the oven to 375 degrees.

3 **To make the topping:** Measure the flour, polenta or cornmeal, nuts, brown sugar, and cinnamon into the bowl of a food processor and pulse a few times. Add the pieces of butter and pulse until the butter is finely broken up. Continue to pulse until the crisp topping no longer looks sandy and is just beginning to hold together.

4 Scatter all of the crisp topping evenly over the fruit filling. Bake the crisp for about 50 minutes, until the topping is nicely browned and the fruit is fully cooked. Poke a sharp knife into the center; if it meets no resistance, the crisp is done.

BUCKWHEAT CAKE WITH APPLES POACHED IN CIDER

ONE 9-INCH CAKE

THE BUCKWHEAT CAKE:

1½ cups sliced almonds

½ cup buckwheat flour

1 teaspoon baking powder

12 tablespoons (1½ sticks) unsalted butter, at room temperature

½ cup plus 6 tablespoons sugar

1 teaspoon vanilla extract

4 large eggs, at room temperature, separated

¼ teaspoon salt

Optional: ¼ teaspoon cream of tartar

THE APPLES POACHED IN CIDER:

3 cups apple cider or unsweetened apple juice

½ cup sugar

1 cinnamon stick

5 whole cloves

2 to 3 firm apples (Granny Smith or Golden Delicious)

Optional: Powdered sugar

My most excellent pastry buddy Mary Jo Thoresen of Jojo restaurant in Oakland, California, passed along this recipe for an unusual and most excellent cake. Mary Jo and I used to joke so often and laugh so hard when we worked together that the chef would have to come over and reprimand us as if we were two little children.

The suggested accompaniment of poached apple balls puts to perfect use the melon baller that you've had in the back of the drawer and were wondering what the heck you would ever use it for! They are at their best made a day in advance, refrigerated, and rewarmed before serving. The apple balls are also good with polenta cake (page 46) and with frozen caramel mousse (page 39).

1   Position a rack in the center of the oven and preheat the oven to 350 degrees. Butter a 9 by 2-inch round cake pan and line the bottom with a circle of parchment paper.

2   **To make the buckwheat cake:** In a food processor, pulse the almonds with the buckwheat flour and baking powder until the almonds are finely ground.

3   In the bowl of an electric mixer, or by hand, beat together the butter and ½ cup sugar until very light and fluffy, 3 to 5 minutes if using a mixer. Beat in the vanilla and the egg yolks, one at a time, scraping the sides of the bowl as necessary.

4   In a separate metal or glass bowl, whip the egg whites until they become frothy. Add the salt and cream of tartar (if using) and continue to whip until the whites begin to hold their shape. Gradually whip in the 6 tablespoons of sugar and keep whipping until the whites form soft, shiny peaks.

5   Blend the almond and buckwheat mixture into the creamed butter and egg-yolk mixture with a rubber spatula. Stir about a third of the beaten egg whites into the batter. (It will be thick, but this will lighten it up.) Then carefully fold in the remaining egg whites until just incorporated. Don't overfold!

6   Transfer the batter to the prepared cake pan, smooth the top, and bake for 45 minutes, until a toothpick inserted into the center comes out clean. Cool on wire rack.

7   **To poach the apples:** Warm the cider, sugar, and spices in a medium saucepan. Peel the apples with a vegetable peeler and use a $\frac{1}{2}$-inch melon baller to make apple balls.

8   Drop the apple balls into the cider mixture and simmer gently for 10 minutes, or until just tender.

Serving: Dust cake with powdered sugar, if desired. Serve the cake with the warm apple balls and a spoonful of their syrup. Instead of the apple balls, you might also top the cake with orange segments drizzled with honey or with sautéed cherries (page 167).

Note: This cake will keep beautifully for 5 days, well wrapped, at room temperature.

APPLE TART WITH WHOLE-WHEAT EXPRESS PUFF PASTRY AND MAPLE-WALNUT SAUCE

8 SERVINGS

THE WHOLE-WHEAT
EXPRESS PUFF PASTRY:
(enough for 2 tarts)

1 pound (4 sticks)
unsalted butter

2 cups all-purpose flour

¼ cup whole-wheat flour

1 teaspoon salt

¾ cup ice water

THE TART:

3 medium-size apples
(1½ pounds)

1½ tablespoons butter,
melted

1 tablespoon sugar

THE MAPLE-WALNUT
SAUCE: (about 1½ cups
sauce)

2 tablespoons butter,
salted or unsalted

½ cup firmly packed light
brown sugar

5 tablespoons pure maple
syrup

2 tablespoons water

½ cup walnuts, toasted

¼ teaspoon ground
cinnamon

1 teaspoon bourbon

When I left the restaurant business, I thought I would never want to make puff pastry again. Although many bakeries or restaurants have a large machine that effortlessly rolls puff pastry dough, I never had the luxury of working in such a place.

However, ever since my colleague Linda Zagula came up with an "express" puff pastry that's so simple to do it basically involves about fifteen minutes of work, I find I'm climbing aboard the puff pastry express whenever I feel like it. The version I've created is for a whole-wheat express pastry, which is a bit more rustic than traditional puff pastry. I love it with apples. And I like the sound of "whole-wheat express." It has a healthy ring to it that makes me feel slightly better about making my guests eat that much butter all at once.

When you make the dough, you will wonder at first how it could ever become smooth, but after the first couple of foldings, you'll see the dough come together, smooth and supple, and you'll feel like a pro.

I always make twice the amount I need, so I can freeze the other half and use it later.

1 **To make the whole-wheat puff pastry:** Cut the butter into ½-inch cubes, distribute them evenly over a dinner plate or baking sheet, separating them with your fingers, and freeze for at least 1 hour.

2 In the bowl of an electric mixer, stir together the all-purpose and whole-wheat flours and salt. Add the frozen butter cubes, and mix at low speed for about 1 minute, until the but-

ter's sharp edges are curved (that's how Linda describes it). Add the ice water and mix until the flour absorbs it; the dough will look very ragged, with large pieces of butter relatively intact.

3   Turn the dough out onto a lightly floured countertop. Knead with your hands a few times, then shape the dough with a rolling pin and your hands into a 10-by-15-inch rectangle. (The dough will not be at all smooth at this point, which is normal; don't expect a perfect rectangle.) Press inward with the heel of your hand to flatten the edges and approximate the dough into a rectangular shape. During the entire dough-rolling process, whenever it sticks you'll need to lightly flour the top of the dough and the countertop beneath it. Avoid using too much flour, and brush away any excess.

4   With the long side parallel to the edge of the countertop, fold the dough into thirds. First fold the right-hand third over the center, then fold the left third over to cover it. Rotate the dough a quarter-turn clockwise, so the seam is facing you.

5   Lightly flour the countertop and roll out the dough a second time into a rectangle about the same size as before, about 10 by 15 inches. Once again, fold the right third of the dough over the center, and fold the left third over that. The seams should be evenly aligned; if they aren't, unfold the dough and refold it so they are parallel. Again rotate the dough clockwise a quarter-turn, so the seam is facing you.

6   For the third time, roll out the dough into a rectangle, folding the dough as before, and rotate the dough clockwise a quarter-turn.

7   Roll out the dough into a rectangle for a fourth time, fold as before, wrap the dough in plastic wrap, and refrigerate for at least 2 hours.

8   Remove the dough from the refrigerator and roll it out into a rectangle for a fifth time. Fold it in thirds as before and roll it once more into a rectangle (this is the sixth time). Fold it in thirds as before, wrap in plastic, and chill until ready to use.

9   Position an oven rack in the center of the oven and preheat the oven to 400 degrees. Line a baking sheet with parchment paper.

10   **To make the tart:** Cut the chilled dough in half, reserving one half (see Note below), and on a lightly floured surface roll out the other into a 12-by-15-inch rectangle. Transfer the dough rectangle to the parchment-lined baking sheet. If you wish, brush water around the edge of the rectangle and crimp or fold the dough over on itself to make a decorative fluted rim. With a fork prick the bottom of the dough all over about 25 times.

11   Peel, quarter, and core the apples, and slice them into $\frac{1}{4}$-inch-thick slices. Arrange the apples on the puff pastry in overlapping rows. Brush the apples with the melted butter and sprinkle with the tablespoon of sugar.

12   Bake the tart about 35 minutes, until the apples are cooked and beginning to brown. Slide the tart off the baking sheet onto a large cooking rack.

13   **To make the maple-walnut sauce:** Bring the butter, brown sugar, maple syrup, and water to a full boil in a small saucepan. Boil for 30 seconds and remove from the heat.

14   Coarsely chop the walnuts. Stir them into the sauce along with the cinnamon and bourbon.

Serving: Serve a square of the tart with a generous spoonful of the maple-walnut sauce.

Note: The reserved puff pastry can be wrapped in plastic, then foil, and frozen for up to 3 months. Defrost overnight in the refrigerator before rolling out. Or keep the reserved dough in the fridge, but for no more than a day or two—longer than that and it starts to turn gray.

SPICED APPLE CHARLOTTE WITH CIDER SABAYON

6 TO 8 SERVINGS

THE CHARLOTTE:

8 medium-size apples
(3 pounds), peeled,
quartered, and cored

½ teaspoon ground
cinnamon

½ teaspoon freshly grated
nutmeg

⅛ teaspoon ground cloves

½ cup water

6 tablespoons plus 1 tablespoon sugar

1 teaspoon vanilla extract

4 tablespoons (½ stick)
unsalted butter, melted

12 slices of firm-textured
white bread (about ¾
pound), such as *pain
de mie*

THE SABAYON:

⅓ cup sugar

½ cup sparkling apple
cider

¼ cup applejack or
Calvados

6 large egg yolks

Optional: ½ cup heavy
cream, softly whipped

To me, peeling apples is one of the most Zen-like tasks there is. You enter an alert meditative state in which you can enjoy the subtle variations that make each apple unlike any other. And although some bakers recommend it, I never use acidulated water to keep my apple slices from oxidizing and discoloring a little. If they're going to be cooked, there's really no reason to: They're going to get colored anyway.

Use a very good baking apple such as Pippin, Jonathan, Gravenstein, Sierra Beauty, Cortland, or Rome Beauty.

1   To make the charlotte: Dice the apples into ¼-inch pieces. Put them in a medium-size saucepan and add the cinnamon, nutmeg, cloves, and water. Cover and cook over medium heat for about 5 minutes, stirring occasionally, until the apples are heated through. Remove the lid, stir in 6 tablespoons sugar, and cook until the apples form a thick purée the consistency of mashed potatoes. (Some apples will take longer to cook, or be more juicy, so the cooking time will vary.) Once the apples are cooked, remove from the heat and stir in the vanilla.

2   Slide the oven rack into its lowest position and preheat the oven to 375 degrees.

3   To assemble the charlotte, generously butter the sides of a 2-quart soufflé dish or charlotte mold. Sprinkle 1 tablespoon of sugar in the dish and tilt to coat the bottom and the sides.

4   Trim the edges from the slices of bread. Cut some of the bread into pieces that will fit snugly into the bottom of the soufflé dish. (I find it easiest to cut square slices of bread diag-

onally into triangles, and then fit them into the bottom of the dish in a pinwheel pattern.) Butter the sides of the bread that face down and arrange the pieces in the bottom of the baking dish. Tightly line the sides of the baking dish with more bread, buttering the sides facing outward.

5   Spoon the apple purée into the bread-lined baking dish and top with the remaining slices of bread. Butter the top and trim any slices of bread that protrude above the top of the dish.

6   Bake the charlotte for 35 minutes. Let cool 15 minutes, then set a serving plate on top and invert the charlotte onto it to release it. Remove the dish.

7   **To make the sabayon:** In a large heatproof bowl, whisk together the sugar, cider, and applejack or Calvados. Whisk in the egg yolks. Set the bowl over a saucepan of simmering water and whisk vigorously until the mixture becomes light and frothy and holds its shape when you lift the whisk. Immediately fold in the whipped cream (if using) and serve. If you wish to serve the sabayon later, set the whipped sabayon in a bowl of ice and stir until cool. Serve immediately, or it can be refrigerated for up to 1 day ahead of serving.

Serving: Cut the warm charlotte into wedges and serve with a spoonful of the sabayon.

Variation: For a caramelized apple charlotte, omit buttering and sugaring the baking dish. Instead, caramelize 1 cup of sugar (following the instructions for caramelizing in step 5 for pineapple flan on page 69). Once it's caramelized, stop the cooking by adding ⅓ cup water and 1 tablespoon lemon juice, being careful (and wearing an oven mitt), or the caramel will bubble up and splatter. Pour the warm caramel into the unbuttered soufflé dish or charlotte mold, carefully tilting the dish to coat the sides with the caramel. Let cool until firm. Line the baking dish with buttered bread slices, then fill and bake the charlotte on the center rack of the oven for 30 minutes.

APPLE AND QUINCE TARTE TATIN

ONE 10-INCH TART, 8 SERVINGS

THE DOUGH:

¾ cup flour

2 teaspoons sugar

¼ teaspoon salt

4 tablespoons (½ stick) unsalted butter, cut into ½-inch pieces and chilled

2½ tablespoons ice water

THE FRUIT FILLING:

2 quinces (about 1 pound), peeled, cored, seeded, and cut into ¼-inch-thick slices

8 medium-size apples (about 4 pounds), peeled, quartered, and cored

3 tablespoons unsalted butter

¾ cup sugar

Crème fraîche or vanilla ice cream, for serving

At a recent culinary conference, I was excited to find that our table centerpieces were composed of stunningly exotic fruits from around the world. I immediately pushed my mediocre dinner aside, rolled up my sleeves, and, much to the surprise of my tablemates, sliced up all the fruits in the arrangement. All except for the quinces, that is, which should not be eaten raw. (Them I pocketed and took home, where they could release their exquisite fragrant aroma as they cooked.) Use care when you cut up a quince; the flesh is dense and hard even when ripe, and it can be difficult to cut out the core. Try cutting the quince in half and using a melon baller to take out the core and the membranes around it.

1   **To make the dough:** Mix together the flour, sugar, and salt, using an electric mixer or a pastry blender.

2   Add the cut-up chilled butter and keep mixing until the butter pieces are somewhat broken up but still very chunky. Add the ice water and mix until the dough comes together. Gather the dough and shape it into a disk, wrap it in plastic, and refrigerate for at least 30 minutes.

3   **To make the fruit filling:** Caramelize the apples and quince: First melt the 3 tablespoons butter in a well-seasoned 10-inch cast-iron skillet (or a large, nonreactive frying pan). Sprinkle the ¾ cup sugar over the bottom of the pan and remove from the heat.

4   Pack the apple quarters into the pan, standing them on end. It may seem like a lot of apples, but they'll cook down. Insert the quince slices among the apple sections.

5   Place the pan on the stovetop and cook over medium heat for about 25 minutes, until the juices thicken and become slightly caramelized. (You may want to lift an apple once in a while to make sure the apples are not darkening too much on the bottom.) Remove from the heat.

6   Position the oven rack in the lower third of the oven and preheat the oven to 375 degrees.

7   On a lightly floured surface, roll out the dough into a 12-inch circle. Drape the dough over the apples in the skillet and tuck the edges down between the sides of the skillet and the apples.

8   Bake the tart for 40 minutes, until the dough is browned. Remove from the oven and carefully invert onto a large serving plate. (Wear oven mitts and tilt the plate and skillet away from you to prevent any hot juice from spilling on you.)

Serving: Cut the tart into wedges and serve warm, with crème fraîche or vanilla ice cream.

Note: Poaching the quince before assembling the tart will make them turn a lovely ruby red and bring out extra flavor: Heat $\frac{1}{2}$ cup sugar with $1\frac{1}{2}$ cups water and a 2-inch piece of vanilla bean, split lengthwise. Peel, core, and cut the quince into eighths. Put them in the saucepan, cover with a circle of parchment paper cut to fit inside the pan, and simmer, covered, for 30 to 60 minutes, until the quince are tender. Once poached, the quince can be kept in the refrigerator for up to 10 days. Poached quinces are good by themselves, in fruit compotes and other tarts, and as an alternative accompaniment to cakes such as the buckwheat cake on page 21.

QUINCE MARMALADE WITH MANCHEGO CHEESE

ABOUT 3 CUPS

1 pound quince (about 3)

3 cups sugar

4 cups water

½ lemon

Manchego cheese

This simple pairing of quince preserves and Spanish cheese with a glass of cold sherry will make you feel as if you're in an old-fashioned Andalusian *bodega*—a wine shop with big casks of Amontillado and Manzanilla behind a little bar over which hang wineskins, ropes of garlic, and hams tied up by their little black hoofs still attached. Quince marmalade is good for breakfast, too—without the sherry, of course.

This marmalade was inspired by one of Helen Witty's recipes in her regrettably out-of-print cookbook, *Fancy Pantry.*

1   Quarter and peel the quince and remove the cores and seeds. Shred the quince on the large holes of a metal grater.

2   Bring the sugar and water to a boil in a large saucepan. Add the grated quince and the lemon half, and cook over medium heat at a slow boil, until the mixture is thick. This should take at least 30 minutes. (It should register 220 degrees on a candy thermometer. Or test it by putting a spoonful on a well-chilled plate; it should gel enough that it wrinkles when nudged with your finger.)

3   Remove the lemon half and transfer the marmalade to a clean jar until ready to serve.

Serving: Slice the Manchego cheese into relatively thin slices. Arrange them on a dessert plate, add a dollop of the marmalade, and let each diner spread a bit of the marmalade on the cheese slices. Serve with glasses of chilled sherry.

Note: Quince marmalade is marvelous as a cake filling, sandwiched between two layers of lemony sponge cake.

STILTON SHORTCAKES WITH CANDIED PECANS AND HONEY-POACHED PEARS

THE CANDIED PECANS:

I large egg white (save the yolk for glazing the biscuits)

½ cup firmly packed light brown sugar

2 tablespoons ground cinnamon

I teaspoon ground ginger

I teaspoon ground cloves

I teaspoon cayenne

½ teaspoon salt

2 teaspoons vanilla extract

4 cups pecan halves (or walnut halves or almonds)

THE HONEY-POACHED PEARS:

2 cups water

⅔ cup honey

4 wide strips of lemon zest

3 ripe, firm pears (such as Bosc), peeled, cored, and quartered

THE STILTON SHORT-CAKES:

2 cups flour

I tablespoon sugar

2 teaspoons baking powder

¼ teaspoon salt

Shortcake is a dessert biscuit that's almost always associated with summertime strawberries, so a winterized shortcake like this one is a little unexpected. People don't expect to find bits of blue cheese in their dessert, either, but don't forget Stilton is a classic dessert cheese all by itself.

If you don't want to make the shortcakes, the honey-poached pears would be delicious served warm over chocolate or caramel ice cream.

The candied pecan recipe makes more than you will need for serving with the shortcake, but I'm sure the extra ones won't be wasted as they are terrific for nibbling. I often make a batch for impromptu gift-giving, for snacking on with cocktails, and for mixing into salads.

1   Preheat the oven to 300 degrees.

2   **To candy the pecans:** In a large bowl, mix the egg white with the brown sugar, spices, cayenne, salt, vanilla, and pecans. Stir until the nuts are well coated.

3   Spray a baking sheet with nonstick spray, and evenly spread the nuts on it. Bake for 30 minutes, stirring every 10 minutes, until the pecans are well toasted and the glaze is dry. Cool completely, separating them as they cool. Set aside a handful to chop and sprinkle on the finished shortcakes. Store the remaining pecans in an airtight container for up to 2 weeks.

4   **To poach the pears:** In a nonreactive large saucepan, heat together the water, honey, and lemon zest. Add the pears, cover with a round of parchment paper cut to fit the pan, and gently simmer until the pears are translucent (a knife should easily pierce all the way through), about 15 minutes. Remove

¼ teaspoon freshly
ground black pepper

4 tablespoons (½ stick)
unsalted butter, cut into
½-inch cubes and chilled

4 ounces Stilton cheese,
crumbled (about 1 cup)

⅔ cup buttermilk

1 egg yolk, for glazing
(reserved from candying
the pecans)

THE WHIPPED CREAM:
(makes 2 cups)

1 cup heavy cream

1 tablespoon sugar

A few drops of vanilla
extract

Variation: Little Stilton
shortcakes also make a
great appetizer or snack.
After you add the butter-
milk, work into the dough
a spoonful or two each of
chopped scallion and
chopped prosciutto or
cooked and crumbled
bacon. Roll or pat out the
dough ¾ inch thick, as
above, but cut out smaller
biscuits. Bake until
golden brown.

the pears with a slotted spoon. Continue to simmer the poaching liquid until thick and syrupy. Reserve.

5   **To make the shortcakes:** Increase the heat of the oven to
400 degrees.

6   Mix together the flour, sugar, baking powder, salt, and
pepper. With an electric mixer, food processor, or pastry
blender mix in the butter and the crumbled Stilton. Mix until
the butter is completely broken up into small pieces. Stir in the
buttermilk.

7   On a lightly floured surface, pat or roll the dough into a
¾-inch-thick sheet. Using a 2½-inch-round biscuit cutter, cut
out as many biscuits as you can. Gather the scraps, knead them
gently and briefly, and roll or pat the dough out again into a
¾-inch-thick sheet. Cut out more biscuits. When they are done,
you should have 8 biscuits in all.

8   Place the biscuits, evenly spaced, on a parchment-
covered baking sheet. Beat the egg yolk with a fork and brush
it over the tops of the biscuits. Bake the biscuits for 18 minutes, until the tops are deep golden brown. Cool on a wire rack.

9   **To make the whipped cream:** Use an electric mixer or a
wire whisk to whip the cream until it just begins to hold a
shape. Whisk in the sugar and vanilla, and continue whipping
until the cream is soft, creamy, and mounding gently.

Serving: Coarsely chop the reserved candied pecans, and slice
the poached pears. Split the biscuits. Place the bottom half of
each biscuit on a dessert plate, and spoon a dollop of whipped
cream over it. Put pear slices on top of the cream and spoon some
of the reduced honey syrup over the pears. Sprinkle with candied
pecans, and cap with the top halves of the biscuits.

Note: The shortcakes are best made and served the same day.

MARSALA-POACHED PEARS STUFFED WITH RICOTTA, CHOCOLATE, ALMONDS, AND CHERRIES

4 SERVINGS

THE PEARS:

2 cups sugar

5 cups water

¾ cup Marsala, dry or sweet

3 strips of lemon zest, each ½ inch wide

4 firm pears (such as Bosc or Winter Nellis)

THE FILLING:

¼ cup dark rum

⅓ cup dried sour cherries

2 ounces bittersweet or semisweet chocolate

¼ cup almonds, toasted

⅔ cup ricotta cheese (part-skim or low-fat)

1 tablespoon sugar

1 tablespoon milk or cream

This dessert was inspired by the flavors of the Italian classic *cassata alla siciliana,* traditionally a kind of ricotta cheesecake flavored with chocolate, nuts, and candied fruit. I had a hunch the same flavors would be wonderful with poached pears, and they were.

1   **To poach the pears:** Bring the sugar, water, Marsala, and lemon zest to a boil in a medium-size saucepan. As the liquid is heating, peel the pears with a vegetable peeler and cut out a shallow cone-shaped, quarter-sized piece from the base of each pear (the blossom end).

2   In a small pan, warm the dark rum and cherries. Remove from the heat, cover, and set aside to plump.

3   Lower the heat under the Marsala poaching liquid. Add the pears, submerge them, and cover with a round of parchment paper cut the same diameter as the saucepan. Gently simmer for 45 minutes to 1 hour (depending on the size of the pears and their ripeness), turning them every so often so they cook evenly. They are done when the tip of a paring knife goes in easily. Remove the pears and stand them upright on a plate to cool. (Or they can cool in the poaching liquid and be left to soak. See Note on page 38.)

4   Increase the heat under the Marsala poaching liquid and reduce it by two-thirds, to the consistency of maple syrup.

5   **To make the filling:** Drain the plumped cherries in a sieve set over a bowl, pressing down to squeeze out most of the liquid. Reserve the liquid and coarsely chop the cherries.

6   Grate the chocolate on the large holes of a metal grater. Finely chop the almonds.

7   Mix together the chopped cherries and their reserved soaking liquid, grated chocolate, almonds, ricotta, and sugar. Add the milk or cream.

8   Dig through the base of each pear with a melon baller and cut out the core. (Or cut the pears in half and cut out the cores.) Hollow out the center of each pear a little more, being careful not to cut through the sides. Use an iced-tea spoon to spoon the ricotta filling into the pears. (Depending on the size of the pears, you may have a small amount left over.) Refrigerate the pears until ready to serve.

Serving: Serve a whole pear per person, with a generous amount of the reduced poaching liquid ladled over it. (Or serve the halves topped with poaching liquid.)

Note: These pears benefit immeasurably from a long soaking in their flavorful poaching liquid. They can be poached several days in advance, then filled and refrigerated up to 8 hours ahead of serving.

FROZEN CARAMEL MOUSSE WITH SHERRY-GLAZED PEARS, CHOCOLATE, AND SALTED ALMONDS

ABOUT 1 QUART FROZEN MOUSSE, ENOUGH PEARS AND ALMONDS FOR 4 TO 5 SERVINGS

THE MOUSSE:

¼ cup plus ¼ cup water

¾ cup granulated sugar

5 large egg yolks

2 tablespoons dark brown sugar

1 teaspoon vanilla extract

¼ teaspoon salt

¾ cup heavy cream

THE SALTED ALMONDS:

½ cup slivered almonds

¼ teaspoon vegetable oil

¼ teaspoon coarse salt

THE SHERRY-GLAZED PEARS AND SAUCE:

2 firm, ripe pears (such as Bosc, d'Anjou, or Bartlett), peeled and cored

⅓ cup sherry

2 tablespoons light brown sugar

Optional: A pinch of ground anise seed

3 ounces bittersweet or semisweet chocolate, chopped into ¼-inch pieces

My favorite sherry story is told by Marion Cunningham, who once wrote a recipe for a newspaper that called for "dry sherry." Soon after, an irate woman called the paper to complain that she had looked everywhere and powdered sherry was absolutely just impossible to find.

Just so you know, there are sweet and dry sherries and both come in liquid form. Either works well in this recipe.

1   **To make the mousse:** Pour ¼ cup of water into a medium-size unlined skillet or saucepan, then sprinkle the granulated sugar over it in an even layer. Set the pan over moderate heat and cook, without stirring, until the sugar melts and begins to darken at the edges. Tilt the pan gently once or twice, if necessary, to encourage even browning.

2   While the sugar is cooking, begin whipping together the egg yolks and the dark brown sugar in an electric mixer on high speed.

3   Once the sugar has caramelized (it should be dark brown and smoking, but should not smell burnt) remove from the heat, and add the remaining ¼ cup of water. Wear an oven mitt and take care, as the mixture will sputter when you add the water. As the bubbles subside, stir to melt any hardened caramel.

4   Once the egg yolks and brown sugar mixture are light and fluffy, with the mixer still on high speed, slowly drizzle in the caramel; you should be pouring so slowly that it takes about 2 minutes to pour it all in. (Avoid pouring the caramel

directly over the beaters, which will cause the caramel to splash onto the sides of the bowl instead of being incorporated into the egg yolks.)

5   Continue to whip the mixture until it cools to room temperature. Mix in the vanilla extract and salt.

6   In a separate bowl, whip the cream until it just forms firm peaks; it should not be grainy.

7   Fold the whipped cream into the caramel-egg mixture. Transfer to another large bowl, or a container with a lid, and freeze the mousse for at least 6 hours.

8   Preheat the oven to 350 degrees.

9   **To make the salted almonds:** Toss the almonds with the oil and coarse salt. Spread on a baking sheet and bake, stirring occasionally, until the almonds are well roasted, about 13 minutes.

10   **To make the sherry-glazed pears and sauce:** Increase the oven to 400 degrees.

11   Cut the pears into quarters and put in a shallow baking dish. Toss with the sherry and light brown sugar. Add the anise seed, if you wish. Cover with foil and bake the pears for 30 minutes.

12   Remove the pears from the oven, drain off the cooking juices into a separate container, and stir in the bittersweet chocolate until it has melted completely.

Note: Leftover chocolate sauce can be covered and stored in the refrigerator for up to 10 days; the mousse can be frozen for up to 1 month, if well covered.

Serving: Divide the pears among the serving plates. Spoon a mound of the frozen caramel mousse over the pears, drizzle with chocolate sauce, and sprinkle with salted almonds.

CORNMEAL SHORTCAKES WITH
SPICE-BAKED PEARS

6 SERVINGS

THE PEARS:

4 firm, ripe pears (such as Bosc or d'Anjou), peeled, cored, and cut into 6 slices each

6 tablespoons dark brown sugar

½ cup apricot preserves

½ teaspoon ground cinnamon

2 tablespoons fresh lemon juice

1½ tablespoons water

THE SHORTCAKES:

1¼ cups all-purpose flour

½ cup stone-ground yellow cornmeal

3 tablespoons sugar

1¼ teaspoons baking powder

¼ teaspoon baking soda

½ teaspoon salt

6 tablespoons (¾ stick) unsalted butter, cut into ½-inch pieces and chilled

6 tablespoons buttermilk

1 large egg, beaten

1½ cups whipped cream (page 35)

This is a considerably leaner version of a traditional shortcake, especially if you forgo the whipped cream. Frozen yogurt would be a good substitute.

A baker friend of mine, Manï, came over once while I was baking and was absolutely horrified to see that I wasn't using stone-ground cornmeal. He then gave me a stern lecture about why I should use stone-ground. I've followed his advice, and I must say, I've become a convert; the superiority in both flavor and texture is amazing.

1   Position an oven rack in the center of the oven and pre-heat the oven to 400 degrees. Line a baking sheet with parchment paper.

2   **To make the shortcakes:** Mix together the flour, corn-meal, sugar, baking powder, baking soda, and salt in a food processor. Add the pieces of butter and pulse until all the butter is in small pea-size pieces. Add the buttermilk and pulse until the dough just comes together.

3   On a lightly floured surface, roll out or pat the dough ¾ inch thick. With a 3-inch round biscuit cutter, cut 4 biscuits. Gather the scraps and roll or pat out the dough again into a ¾-inch-thick sheet. Cut out 2 more biscuits.

4   Place the biscuits, evenly spaced, on the prepared baking sheet. Brush the tops of the biscuits with the beaten egg, and bake for 15 to 20 minutes, until golden brown. Cool briefly on a wire rack.

5   **To prepare the pears:** Put the pear slices in a shallow 2-quart baking dish. Toss with the brown sugar, preserves, cinnamon, lemon juice, and water. Cover with foil and bake the pears for 30 minutes, stirring once during baking. Remove from the oven and cool to room temperature.

Serving: Split the biscuits in half. Put a dollop of whipped cream on the bottom halves, top with some of the pear slices, drizzle with the pear cooking liquid, and place the remaining biscuit halves on top.

Note: The biscuits are best eaten shortly after baking, still warm if you like, but you can bake the pears earlier in the day or even the night before.

Variation: For cornmeal shortcakes with spice-baked pears and cranberries, add $\frac{2}{3}$ cup dried cranberries to the pear slices before baking.

PEAR, CHERRY, AND CHOCOLATE BREAD PUDDING

THE PUDDING:

⅓ cup dried sour cherries

⅓ cup brandy or cognac

½ tablespoon unsalted butter

2 pears, peeled, cored, and diced into ½-inch pieces

1 tablespoon brown sugar

4 cups bread cubes, in ¾-inch pieces

4 ounces bittersweet or semisweet chocolate, broken into roughly ½-inch pieces, or ⅔ cup chocolate chips

2 cups milk

1 cup heavy cream

3 large eggs

½ cup plus 2 tablespoons sugar

½ teaspoon almond extract

1 teaspoon ground cinnamon

THE SAUCE:
(makes 2 cups)

4 cups apple juice or cider

⅔ cup granulated sugar

2 tablespoons butter

I have nothing against restaurants, but bread pudding has to be homemade for me to want it. Who wants to go out to eat leftover bread at a fancy restaurant? I've added roasted pears, sour cherries, and, because I couldn't resist a little luxury, bits of melted bittersweet chocolate. Although you can use chocolate chips, broken-up bittersweet chocolate rewards you with runny and irregular pockets of chocolate. So why go out for comfort food, when it's meant to be enjoyed comfortably at home?

1   **To make the bread pudding:** Plump the dried cherries in the brandy or cognac.

2   Melt the butter in a medium-size skillet. Add the diced pears and brown sugar and cook over medium-high heat, stirring occasionally, until the pears are browned, about 10 minutes. Set aside to cool.

3   Position the oven rack in the center of the oven and preheat the oven to 325 degrees. Lightly butter a shallow 2-quart baking dish.

4   In a large mixing bowl, toss together the browned pears, bread cubes, chocolate pieces, the cherries, and their soaking liquid.

5   In another bowl, make a custard mixture by whisking together the milk, cream, eggs, ½ cup sugar, almond extract, and cinnamon.

6   Distribute the bread and fruit mixture evenly in the baking dish. Pour the custard mixture over the bread. Press down on the bread so it can soak in the custard. Sprinkle the remaining 2 tablespoons of sugar over the top.

7   Bake the pudding for 40 to 45 minutes, until lightly browned but still jiggly in the middle. Cool slightly before serving.

8   **To make the sauce:** While the bread pudding is baking, simmer the apple juice and granulated sugar together until reduced to about 2 cups, about 30 minutes. Stir in the butter.

Serving: Serve a warm mound of the bread pudding with a generous soaking of the warm sauce.

Variation: Add 4 ounces of finely crumbled almond paste to the bread, chocolate, and fruit mixture.

POLENTA CAKE WITH SAFFRON-POACHED PEARS

ONE 10-INCH CAKE, 10 SERVINGS

THE CAKE:

1 tablespoon unsalted butter, very soft, for pan

2 teaspoons finely minced fresh rosemary leaves

2 tablespoons plus ¾ cup yellow cornmeal, preferably stone-ground

1 cup flour

2 teaspoons baking powder

¾ teaspoon salt

12 tablespoons (1½ sticks) unsalted butter, at room temperature

1⅓ cups sugar

¼ cup olive oil

5 large eggs, at room temperature

2 large egg yolks

1 teaspoon almond or vanilla extract

3 ounces candied angelica, minced, or 4 teaspoons minced fresh rosemary leaves

A 1927 cookbook I have called *Anyone Can Bake* asserts flatly that although olive oil is "delicious in salad dressings and for frying, [it] is not satisfactory for cakes." After trying this polenta cake, I think you'll agree with me that tastes have changed.

The saffron-flavored pears that go along with it were inspired by a surfeit of saffron that I brought back from a trip to Morocco, where I went searching for spices in souks. In the spice medinas, turmeric, cumin, and paprika were majestically lined up in conical piles, all dazzlingly vivid reds and sweet pungent scents. After I was seated and refreshed with a glass of the ubiquitous mint tea, the vendor reached into a small satchel and extricated a few tiny packets of saffron for me to smell.

They cost about the equivalent of a dollar each, so of course I took advantage of him and stocked up. What a bargain, I thought. It wasn't until I got home that I figured out that at Moroccan prices each packet should have cost me about a dime.

1   Smear the butter all over the inside of a 10-cup tube or bundt pan. Sprinkle the rosemary evenly over the inside and dust with 2 tablespoons of cornmeal, tilting the pan to coat the entire inside.

2   Position an oven rack in the center of the oven and preheat the oven to 350 degrees.

3   **To make the cake:** Sift together the flour, remaining ¾ cup cornmeal, baking powder, and salt. Either by hand or in the bowl of an electric mixer, beat the butter and sugar until light and fluffy, 3 to 5 minutes with a mixer.

½ cup honey

3 cups water

25 saffron threads

2 strips of fresh lemon zest, each about 1 inch wide

3 Bosc pears, peeled, quartered, and cored

4   In a separate bowl, stir together the olive oil, eggs, egg yolks, and almond or vanilla extract.

5   While the mixer is running, slowly dribble the egg mixture, a little at a time, into the butter mixture until the eggs are completely incorporated, scraping the sides of the bowl as necessary. Stir in the dry ingredients and the angelica or rosemary, until just incorporated; do not overmix. Transfer the batter into the prepared cake pan and smooth the top. Bake the cake for 40 minutes, until a toothpick inserted in the center comes out clean. Cool on a wire rack for 20 minutes, then invert onto a cake plate.

6   **To make the saffron-poached pears:** In a medium-size nonreactive saucepan, bring the honey and water to a boil. Add the saffron and lemon zest.

7   Cut the pears lengthwise into 1-inch slices. Reduce the heat to a simmer, add the pears, and cook gently in the simmering liquid for 10 minutes. Press the pears down tenderly with a spoon to keep them moist while they're cooking, or cover with a circle of parchment paper. Remove from the heat and set aside until ready to serve. Or refrigerate for up to 3 days, rewarming before serving.

Serving: Serve a slice of the cake with a helping of the warm pears and a spoonful of their poaching syrup. The cake is also great doused with chocolate sauce (page 93).

RHUBARB TART WITH ALMOND NOUGATINE

ONE 9-INCH TART, 8 TO 10 SERVINGS

THE DOUGH:

6 tablespoons (¾ stick) unsalted butter, chilled

½ cup sugar

2 large egg yolks (reserve the whites for the nougatine topping)

1¼ cups flour

½ teaspoon salt

THE FILLING:

2 pounds rhubarb stalks (about 6), trimmed of leaves and root ends

2 tablespoons butter

½ cup sugar

1 teaspoon vanilla extract

THE ALMOND NOUGATINE:

2 large egg whites

¼ cup firmly packed light brown sugar

½ teaspoon ground cinnamon

1½ cups sliced almonds

Optional: 2 cups vanilla ice cream or 2 cups whipped cream (page 35), flavored with a splash of Grand Marnier

The almond topping here was inspired by the apple nougat tart found in many pâtisseries in Paris. The rhubarb filling was inspired by my lifelong affection for rhubarb. When I was a kid, my first introduction to rhubarb—like many people's—was backyard-grown stalks of the stuff dipped in sugar and chewed up raw. (Just the stalks, mind you: The leaves are toxic.) I've liked it ever since, although now I prefer it cooked.

1   **To make the dough:** Cut the butter into 1-inch pieces and let stand at room temperature for 10 minutes. Butter the bottom of a 9-inch springform pan.

2   With an electric mixer or by hand, beat the butter with the sugar until no visible lumps of butter remain. Beat in the egg yolks. Add the flour and salt and mix at low speed until the dough begins to come together.

3   Gather the dough and press it evenly over the bottom and halfway up the sides of the prepared pan. Use the heel of your hand. (Dust your hands with a bit of flour if the dough is sticking to them.) Put the pan in the freezer for at least 30 minutes.

4   **To make the filling:** Slice the rhubarb stalks lengthwise, then cut them crosswise into ¼-inch pieces.

5   Heat 1 tablespoon of the butter in a medium-size skillet. Add half the rhubarb and ¼ cup of the sugar and cook over medium heat, stirring frequently, until the rhubarb breaks down into a chunky paste. The rhubarb pieces should all be

completely cooked through. Transfer the rhubarb to a bowl and cook the remaining half of the rhubarb with the remaining butter and sugar in the same way. Add to the cooked rhubarb in the bowl and stir in the vanilla.

6   Position the oven rack in the center of the oven and pre-heat the oven to 375 degrees.

7   Remove the springform pan from the freezer and line with foil. Pour in a single layer of pie weights, dried beans, or raw rice. Bake the dough for 20 minutes. Remove the pie weights and foil and bake for 5 to 10 minutes more, until the dough is browned. Remove from the oven and cool on a wire rack. Do not turn off the oven.

8   When the tart shell has cooled, spread the rhubarb filling in it.

9   **To make the almond nougatine:** Beat together the egg whites, brown sugar, and cinnamon with a fork. Stir in the almonds. Spread the nougatine evenly over the tart.

10   Bake the tart for 40 minutes, until the nougatine is crisp and browned. Cool the tart on a wire rack for 15 minutes. To serve, remove the sides of the springform pan.

Serving: Serve this tart with vanilla ice cream or Grand Marnier-flavored whipped cream, or simply by itself.

Variation: To make a rhubarb and raspberry tart, stir 1 cup of raspberries into the cooked rhubarb before baking.

Whenever I'm in the mood to go a little crazy, I create a tropical dessert. Tropical fruits may be at home at our local markets, but they still seem wild and daring. Slice open a golden, tangy pineapple, seed a sublimely ripe papaya, or juice a spritzy passion fruit for a quick trip to a latitude without attitude.

TROPICAL FRUITS

PAPAYA CAKE WITH COCONUT GLAZE

ONE 9-INCH ROUND CAKE, 8 TO 10 SERVINGS

THE CAKE:

4 cups papaya chunks
(1 medium papaya, about
1½ pounds)

½ cup water

½ cup cashews, toasted, or
½ cup peeled pistachios

2 rings (3 ounces) dried
pineapple

2 tablespoons rum

1¾ cups flour

1½ teaspoons baking
powder

½ teaspoon salt

½ teaspoon ground
cinnamon

½ teaspoon freshly grated
nutmeg

6 tablespoons (¾ stick)
unsalted butter, at room
temperature

⅔ cup granulated sugar

⅔ cup firmly packed light
brown sugar

3 large eggs, at room
temperature

1 teaspoon vanilla extract

I was feeling (yet another) midlife crisis coming on, so I took a trip to Hawaii and decided to take up surfing. I love the freedom of riding on warm Pacific waves—pretty exotic for a kid from New England. I like tropical beaches and can we talk about the slimming surfer outfit? But being a beginner can be a little brutal as you struggle to get up on the board over and over and over. Good thing I had made a papaya cake with sticky coconutty glaze before I hit the beach my first morning; it was the perfect treat after a day of struggling with the curling surf.

After your grueling days at the beach, you may want to try this cake with coconut ice cream or a tropical sherbet (see the recipe for baked Hawaii, page 55).

1   To make the cake: Peel the papaya and remove the seeds. Cut the flesh into ½-inch pieces (you should have 4 cups of chunks) and put in a nonreactive saucepan with the water. Cover and cook until the papaya is cooked through, about 15 minutes. Purée the chunks of papaya in a blender or food processor.

2   Transfer the papaya purée to the pan and cook, stirring frequently, until reduced to 1 cup. Remove from the heat and cool to room temperature.

3   Coarsely chop the cashews or pistachios. Dice the pineapple into ¼-inch pieces. Toss the pineapple pieces in the rum.

4   Position the oven rack in the center of the oven and preheat the oven to 350 degrees. Butter a bundt pan or tube pan with a volume of 10 to 12 cups.

4 tablespoons butter (½ stick), salted or unsalted

6 tablespoons heavy cream

6 tablespoons firmly packed dark brown sugar

½ cup shredded coconut, sweetened or unsweetened

2 teaspoons dark rum

5   Sift together the flour, baking powder, salt, cinnamon, and nutmeg. Set aside.

6   In the bowl of an electric mixer, or by hand, beat the butter, granulated sugar, and brown sugar together until smooth. Beat in the eggs, one at a time, then the vanilla.

7   Stir in half of the dry ingredients, then the papaya purée. Then stir in the remaining dry ingredients. Mix in the nuts and pineapple pieces.

8   Transfer the batter to the prepared baking pan and bake the cake for 40 minutes, until a toothpick inserted into the center comes out clean. Cool on a wire rack for 15 minutes, then remove the cake from the pan by inverting it onto the cooling rack. Cool completely before glazing.

9   **To make the glaze:** Cut the butter into pieces and heat with the cream and brown sugar in a small saucepan. Bring to a boil and boil for 1 minute. Remove from the heat and stir in the coconut and the rum. Let cool to room temperature. Once cool, spoon the glaze over the cake, encouraging it to run down the sides.

Variation: This cake is also lovely with a chocolate-rum glaze. To make one, melt 4 ounces of chopped bittersweet or semisweet chocolate in a double boiler with 2 tablespoons unsalted butter, 2 tablespoons light corn syrup, and 2 teaspoons rum. Remove from the heat and stir until smooth. Spoon the glaze over the top of the cooled cake, allowing it to run down the sides.

KIWI, PINEAPPLE, AND TOASTED COCONUT BAKED HAWAII

8 TO 12 SERVINGS

THE PINEAPPLE SORBET: (makes 1 pint)

½ fresh pineapple, peeled, cored, and eyes removed

¼ cup sugar

2 teaspoons fresh lime juice

1 teaspoon rum

THE KIWI SORBET: (makes 1 pint)

10 ripe kiwi fruit (about 2 pounds)

½ cup sugar

THE TOASTED COCONUT ICE CREAM: (makes 1 quart)

3 cups half-and-half

¾ cup sugar

1 cup dried coconut, preferably unsweetened, toasted

⅛ teaspoon salt

6 large egg yolks (reserve the whites for the meringue)

½ teaspoon vanilla extract

A tropical baked Alaska? Why not call it a baked Hawaii? After all, it snows at the summit of Mauna Loa! For the true Polynesian experience you can create an active volcano by hollowing out a small lemon or lime half, placing it on top of the assembled baked Hawaii, then smoothing meringue up the sides to cover it. After the baked Hawaii comes out of the oven, fill the lemon half with 80-proof liquor, and carefully ignite just before bringing to the table. Dim the lights first!

The recipe for the toasted coconut ice cream makes about 1 quart, so there will be enough in case you need extra ice cream to fill up the bowl you freeze the baked Hawaii in. If you don't particularly like pineapple or kiwi, you can substitute other compatible fruit sorbets, such as passion fruit, mango, or tangerine.

This recipe is easier than you think. If you follow it step by step, it works perfectly. True, it's labor intensive, but then it's all done before your company shows up. The hardest part of this dessert is finding room in your freezer for it!

1   **To make the pineapple sorbet:** Cut the pineapple into ½-inch pieces. Purée the pineapple pieces in a food processor with the sugar, lime juice, and rum until smooth. Chill thoroughly.

2   **To make the kiwi sorbet:** Peel the kiwi fruit and remove the tough nib at the stem end of each. Purée the kiwi in a food processor with the sugar until smooth. Chill thoroughly. Freeze the kiwi sorbet in your ice cream maker according to the manufacturer's instructions. Once frozen, spread the sorbet evenly into a plastic-lined bowl, then return it to the freezer.

THE MACAROON
LAYER:

¼ cup sliced or slivered almonds

¼ cup flour

½ cup sugar

⅛ teaspoon salt

2 large egg whites

½ cup shredded coconut, sweetened or unsweetened

3 tablespoons rum

THE MERINGUE:

6 large egg whites (reserved from coconut ice cream)

¾ cup sugar

Optional: ¼ teaspoon cream of tartar

I teaspoon vanilla extract

3   **To make the toasted coconut ice cream:** Warm 2 cups of the half-and-half with the sugar, coconut, and salt in a medium-size nonreactive saucepan. Remove from the heat, cover, and let steep for 1 hour.

4   Stir the egg yolks together in a bowl. Gradually add some of the warmed coconut mixture, stirring constantly as you pour. Pour the warmed yolks into the saucepan with the remaining coconut mixture. Place the saucepan over low heat, and cook, stirring constantly and scraping the bottom with a heat-resistant spatula until the custard thickens enough to coat the spatula.

5   Strain the coconut custard through a fine-mesh strainer into the remaining 1 cup of half-and-half and stir in the vanilla. Discard the coconut and chill the custard ice cream mixture thoroughly.

6   To assemble the baked Hawaii, line a 2-quart bowl with plastic wrap and place it in the freezer.

7   Freeze the toasted coconut custard mixture in the ice cream maker. Spread 2 cups of it over the kiwi sorbet, creating a second layer. Reserve the remaining coconut ice cream in the freezer in case you need it to fill the bowl. Return the bowl to the freezer.

8   Finally, freeze the pineapple sorbet in the ice cream maker. Spread it over the coconut ice cream, creating a third layer. Return the bowl to the freezer.

9   Preheat the oven to 350 degrees. Butter a 9-inch pie plate and dust it lightly with flour, tapping out any excess.

10   **To make the macaroon layer:** In a food processor, grind the almonds with the flour, sugar, and salt. Add the egg whites and coconut, and process until just mixed.

11   Spread the macaroon mixture in the prepared pie plate and bake for 22 minutes, until golden brown. Remove from the oven and cool. Once cool, remove the mixture from the pie plate and cut it to fit neatly as the top layer of the baked Hawaii, covering the pineapple sorbet layer. Saturate the macaroon layer with the rum. Freeze until ready to serve, at least 8 hours.

12   **To make the meringue and finish the baked Hawaii:** Position an oven rack so the oven will accommodate the baked Hawaii and preheat the oven to 500 degrees.

13   Beat the egg whites by hand or with an electric mixer until frothy. (Add the cream of tartar, if using.) Once the egg whites just begin to hold their shape, gradually sprinkle in the sugar and keep beating until they are stiff and shiny. Whisk in the vanilla.

14   Unmold the frozen baked Hawaii from the bowl onto an ovenproof serving plate. (You may need to dip the bowl in warm water briefly to help it release.) Use a spatula to swirl the meringue over the entire surface of the baked Hawaii.

15   Place the baked Hawaii in the oven for 3 to 5 minutes, watching carefully until the meringue is pretty thoroughly browned, its pointy tips darkened.

Serving: To serve the baked Hawaii, dip a long serrated knife into a deep pitcher of very hot water and slice the baked Hawaii, dipping the knife into the hot water again before each slice.

MANGO NAPOLEONS WITH LIME CUSTARD AND COCONUT FLATTIES

8 SERVINGS

THE LIME FILLING:
(makes 1¾ cups curd)

½ cup fresh lime juice
(from 4 to 5 limes)

½ cup sugar

¼ cup water

3 large eggs

2 large egg yolks

6 tablespoons (¾ stick)
butter, salted or unsalted,
cut into ½-inch pieces

Grated zest of 2 limes

⅔ cup heavy cream,
whipped with 2 table-
spoons sugar

THE COCONUT
FLATTIES: (makes
about 30 cookies)

¾ cup unsweetened dried
shredded coconut

10 tablespoons sugar

2 teaspoons flour

¼ teaspoon vanilla extract

5 tablespoons butter,
salted or unsalted, melted

2 large egg whites

THE RUM CARAMEL:
(makes ½ cup)

½ cup sugar

¼ cup water

3 tablespoons dark rum

4 large mangoes

This is a fancy dessert, but all of it, save the assembly, can easily be done in advance. I think you'll love the sweet-tart tropical combination of flavors as much as I do. When you do assemble it at the last minute for your guests, you'll make them feel as if they've just dropped a fortune in some high-priced restaurant.

You could simplify the recipe by omitting the rum caramel and simply tossing the mango slices in a bit of sugar—and a shamelessly liberal pour of dark rum.

The coconut flatties—the pastry layer of the napoleons—are so named because, well, they're flat!

1   **To make the lime filling:** In a medium-size nonreactive saucepan, mix together the lime juice, sugar, water, eggs, egg yolks, and butter. Cook over medium heat, stirring constantly with a whisk for a few minutes, until the filling begins to thicken and hold a shape. Remove from the heat and strain through a coarse strainer into a bowl. Stir in lime zest. Chill thoroughly. Once cool, fold in the whipped cream.

2   **To make the coconut flatties:** Thoroughly stir together the coconut, sugar, flour, vanilla, melted butter, and egg whites. Chill for at least 30 minutes.

3   Position the oven rack in the center of the oven and preheat the oven to 350 degrees. Line a baking sheet with parchment paper.

4   Spoon slightly rounded teaspoonfuls of the coconut batter onto the prepared baking sheet, leaving 2 inches of space between each cookie. Dampen your fingers and flatten the mounds slightly. Bake for 10 minutes, rotating the baking sheet midway during baking to ensure even browning.

5   When the cookies are completely brown, remove them from the oven and cool them on the baking sheet. Once the baking sheet is cool, slide a metal spatula under each cookie to remove it from the parchment paper. (Bake the remaining flattie batter on baking sheets that have cooled down completely.)

6   **To make the rum caramel:** Sprinkle the sugar in an even layer in a medium-size heavy-duty skillet. Cook over medium heat. The edges will liquefy and then begin to brown. Stir the melting sugar with a heatproof utensil from time to time, until all the sugar is melted and caramelized to a deep golden brown. It will be gently smoking but not burnt. Immediately add the ½ cup of water to the caramel, wearing an oven mitt and taking precautions not to get splattered. (I pour the water through a wire-mesh colander upturned over the pan.)

7   Once the bubbling has subsided, stir the caramel over low heat to dissolve any bits of unmelted sugar. Stir in the dark rum and allow to cool.

8   To assemble the napoleons, first peel the mangoes and slice the flesh away from the pit on all 4 sides; cut into ⅛-inch-thick slices. Place a heaping tablespoon of the lime filling in the center of a dessert plate. Top with a coconut flattie. Put another heaping tablespoon of the lime filling and a few mango slices on top of the flattie. Top with a second coconut flattie, another dollop of the lime filling, and another mango

slice or two. Top with a final coconut flattie and place a dab of the lime filling on top of that. Scatter more mango slices around the napoleon and drizzle with a tablespoon of the rum caramel.

Variation: Add diced bananas or pineapple to the sliced mangoes.

Note: The lime filling can be made up to 3 days in advance, and the cookies can be baked up to 24 hours in advance and stored at room temperature in an airtight container. The rum caramel will keep at least 2 months in the refrigerator.

MANGO TARTE TATIN WITH CRUSHED
BLACKBERRIES

ONE 10-INCH TART, 8 SERVINGS

THE DOUGH:

¾ cup flour

1½ teaspoons sugar

¼ teaspoon salt

3 tablespoons unsalted butter, cut into 1-inch cubes and chilled

3 tablespoons ice water

THE FILLING:

4 large mangoes, peeled

3 tablespoons unsalted butter

½ cup sugar

¼ teaspoon freshly grated nutmeg

3 tablespoons dark rum

Two 1-pint baskets blackberries

¼ cup sugar

The mango is a relative of the cashew. The relationship is obvious when you compare their elegantly curvaceous shapes. Within each mango is a long seed or pit, which is roughly the same flattened oval shape as the outside of the fruit. I peel mangoes with a sharp paring knife as if I were sculpting. Once they're peeled, the way to cut the flesh off the fruit is by cutting parallel to the large pit within. Since the pit runs lengthwise, balance the peeled mango on its short side and slice down while angling inward, estimating where the pit is.

Years ago I read about the French chef Alain Senderens offering his guests a mango tarte Tatin with mango sorbet. It's such an intriguingly appealing idea that it's been bugging me ever since. When I started work on this book of fruit desserts, I finally tried my hand at coming up with a recipe. It works. I make this tart toward the end of spring, when fragrant mangoes from the tropics are plentiful at the market and the very first blackberries are coming in. If the blackberries are late, another super accompaniment for this tart is the toasted coconut ice cream on page 56.

I   **To make the dough:** Mix together the flour, sugar, and salt. Using an electric mixer or a pastry blender, add the butter and mix until the butter is broken up into pieces the size of corn kernels.

2   Add the ice water and mix until the dough begins to come together. Gather the dough with your hands, shape it into a disk, wrap it in plastic, and refrigerate for at least 30 minutes.

3   **To make the filling:** First peel the mangoes, then cut the flesh from each mango as close to the pit as possible. Slice away the flesh from one flat side of the pit, then from the other flat side. Cut away the remaining flesh on the two short sides. You should get 4 pieces from each mango. Cut the larger pieces in half lengthwise.

4   In a 10-inch skillet (I strongly recommend cast iron), melt the butter with the sugar. Pile the mango slices in the pan and dust them with the nutmeg. Cook over medium-high heat, without stirring, for 20 to 25 minutes, until the bubbling liquid around the mangoes begins to brown. Remove from the heat.

5   Position an oven rack in the lower third of the oven and preheat the oven to 400 degrees.

6   On a lightly floured surface, roll the dough into a 10-inch circle. Drape the dough circle over the mangoes, tucking any overhang next to them. Bake the tart for 30 minutes, until the crust is golden brown. Remove from the oven and carefully invert onto a nonreactive baking sheet or serving platter. Any fruit that has stuck to the pan can be loosened with a fork and reunited with the tart. Sprinkle the dark rum over the warm mangoes.

7   **To crush the blackberries:** Purée half of the berries with the sugar, then strain the purée over the remaining berries.

Serving: Cool the tart briefly before slicing and serving. Serve with a generous spoonful of the crushed blackberries.

Note: The dough can be made up to 3 days in advance and chilled. This tart should be served the day it's baked, however.

PINEAPPLE COCONUT COOKIES

30 TO 35 COOKIES

One 20-ounce can crushed pineapple packed in its own juice

I cup sugar

3½ cups unsweetened dried, shredded coconut

3 large egg whites

½ teaspoon vanilla extract

Crispy outside, creamy-sweet within, these cookies are my current coconut cookie favorite. People who know me might lift an eyebrow at my use of canned pineapple for these, but I say, get over it. Reserve fresh pineapple for the pineapple frangipane tart on page 66.

I　In a large skillet (preferably nonstick), heat the crushed pineapple with its juice and the sugar until the liquid has evaporated. Continue to cook, stirring constantly, until the pineapple gets sticky and begins to stick to the pan and brown. Remove from the heat. You should have about 1¼ cups.

2　In the bowl of a standing electric mixer fitted with the paddle attachment, stir together the coconut and the cooked pineapple. (Or stir the ingredients together in a large bowl.) Stir in the egg whites and vanilla.

3　Position an oven rack in the center of the oven and preheat the oven to 350 degrees. Cover a baking sheet with parchment paper.

4　Form the dough on the prepared baking sheet into 1½-inch-tall pointed mounds, squeezing the dough with your fingertips to form little pyramids.

5　Bake the cookies for about 30 minutes, rotating the baking sheet midway through baking, until the cookies are browned up the sides. (The tips may burn slightly, which is fine.) Let the cookies cool on the baking sheet before serving.

Note: These are best served the day they are made or they will lose some of their crispness. If you must, you can store them for a few days in an airtight container. The dough can be kept refrigerated for up to 5 days and cookies baked as needed.

PINEAPPLE FRANGIPANE TART

8 TO 10 SERVINGS

THE DOUGH:

1¼ cups flour

1 tablespoon sugar

½ teaspoon salt

8 tablespoons (1 stick) unsalted butter, cut into 1-inch pieces and chilled

5 tablespoons ice water

THE FRANGIPANE FILLING:

2 tablespoons plus 2 tablespoons sugar

1 tablespoon rum or kirsch

1 large egg white

⅓ cup almond paste (2½ ounces)

2 tablespoons unsalted butter, at room temperature

½ large, ripe pineapple, peeled, cored, and eyes removed

1 tablespoon unsalted butter, melted

6 tablespoons sliced almonds

THE GLAZE:

1½ cups unsweetened pineapple juice

½ cup sugar

I've been baking this tart a lot since I began teaching across the country, because fresh pineapple is something that is reliably good nationwide and year round. It is undoubtedly one of the most popular recipes that I have ever taught. People look at me kind of funny while I demonstrate making it, which I *think* is because it sounds so unusual. Then, when they taste it, the response is always, "Wow. This *is* great!"

1   **To make the dough:** Mix together the flour, sugar, and salt. With an electric mixer or a pastry blender mix in the butter, mixing until it is broken up but still very chunky.

2   Add the ice water and mix until the dough comes together. Gather the dough and shape it into a disk, wrap it in plastic, and refrigerate for at least 30 minutes.

3   **To make the frangipane filling:** Beat together 2 tablespoons of the sugar with the rum or kirsch, egg white, almond paste, and 2 tablespoons butter. Set aside.

4   Cut the pineapple into ¼-inch-thick slices.

5   Position the oven rack in the center of the oven and preheat the oven to 400 degrees. Line a baking sheet with parchment paper.

6   On a lightly floured surface, roll the dough into a 14-inch circle. Transfer the circle to the prepared baking sheet. Smear two-thirds of the frangipane over the dough, leaving a 1-inch border. Arrange the pineapple slices in an even layer over the frangipane.

7   While rotating the tart, fold the border of dough over onto the pineapple, creating a 1-inch-wide enclosing rim. Evenly distribute dabs of the remaining frangipane on the pineapple.

8   Brush the dough border with the 1 tablespoon of melted butter, spread the almonds evenly over the pineapple, and sprinkle the remaining 2 tablespoons of sugar over the entire tart. (Be generous with the sugar over the crust.)

9   Bake the tart for 40 to 45 minutes, until the crust is golden brown. Remove from the oven and slide the tart onto a cooling rack.

10   **To make the glaze:** While the tart is baking, stir together the pineapple juice and sugar in a skillet. Cook over medium heat until the liquid is reduced to about $\frac{2}{3}$ cup, about 10 minutes.

Serving: Serve a wedge of the tart glazed with a large spoonful of the warm pineapple glaze.

CARAMELIZED PINEAPPLE FLAN

6 SERVINGS

An exceptionally yummy custard. It's flantastic.

THE CUSTARD:

1 cup milk

1 cup half-and-half

½ cup sugar

1 vanilla bean, split lengthwise

4 large eggs

THE PINEAPPLE CARAMEL:

½ fresh pineapple, peeled, cored, and eyes removed (or 2¼ cups canned unsweetened crushed pineapple, drained)

¾ cup sugar

1   To make the custard: Warm the milk, half-and-half, and sugar in a saucepan. Scrape the seeds from the vanilla bean into the warm milk mixture. Add the vanilla bean, remove the pan from the heat, cover, and let steep for 1 hour.

2   Whisk the eggs thoroughly in a mixing bowl. Rewarm the milk and gradually add it to the eggs, whisking constantly as you pour (but not whisking so hard as to make them foam). Strain the custard through a fine-mesh sieve into a large measuring cup or pitcher from which you can pour the custard later. Set aside.

3   To make the pineapple caramel: Dice the fresh pineapple into ¼-inch pieces. In a nonstick skillet cook the pineapple pieces over medium-high heat until dry and cooked through, about 7 minutes. Stir frequently.

4   Once cooked, divide the pineapple evenly among six 4- to 6-ounce ramekins or custard cups, making a single layer. Reserve any remaining pineapple for garnishing the finished custards. Set the ramekins or custard cups in a deep roasting pan.

5   In another skillet, heat the sugar over medium heat, watching it carefully. As soon as the sugar at the edges begins to melt and darken, stir the sugar with a wooden spoon and continue to cook until all the sugar has liquefied and caramelized. It will start to smoke and become a deep amber brown.

6   Immediately pour equal amounts of the caramel over the pineapple in the 6 ramekins or custard cups. Allow the caramel to harden. (See Note on page 70.)

7   To bake the flans, preheat the oven to 350 degrees.

8   Pour the custard into the caramelized 6 ramekins or custard cups. Pour warm water into the roasting pan until it reaches halfway up the sides of the custard cups. Cover the pan snugly with aluminum foil and bake for 50 to 60 minutes, until the flans are just barely set. Remove the flans from the roasting pan and set them on a cooling rack. Once they are cool, refrigerate until ready to serve.

9   To unmold, run a sharp knife around the edge of the chilled custard to release it from the ramekin. Invert a serving plate over the custard, and flip over both the ramekin and the plate simultaneously. Shake gently to release the custard and lift off the ramekin.

Variation: For pineapple coconut flan, steep $\frac{1}{2}$ cup toasted unsweetened coconut in the milk and half-and-half mixture. Strain out the coconut and proceed to step 2.

Notes: The caramel in the bottom of the ramekins should be very hard when you pour in the custard, which should be done right before baking.
   The baked custards can be covered tightly with plastic wrap and kept for up to 3 days in the refrigerator.

BUTTERSCOTCH PUDDING WITH COFFEE-CARAMELIZED BANANAS

THE PUDDING:

4 tablespoons (½ stick) unsalted butter

I cup firmly packed dark brown sugar

I cup heavy cream

2 cups whole milk

¾ teaspoon salt

3 tablespoons cornstarch

2 large eggs

2 teaspoons whiskey

I teaspoon vanilla extract

THE COFFEE-CARAMELIZED BANANAS:

I tablespoon butter

I vanilla bean, split lengthwise

6 tablespoons dark brown sugar

3 bananas, peeled and cut into ½-inch slices

6 tablespoons strong coffee

Years ago, while preparing to make a butterscotch pudding, I telephoned a friend (who shall remain nameless) who worked for a restaurant (also better left nameless) that had been highly praised for its home-style butterscotch pudding. When I asked what they used as a thickener, she replied that they used store-bought butterscotch pudding mix and folded in butterscotch chips!

Try serving the coffee-caramelized bananas with the bittersweet chocolate mousse on page 121.

1   **To make the pudding:** Melt the butter in a medium-size heavy-duty saucepan. Mix in the brown sugar and cook until the mixture bubbles vigorously. Remove from the heat and stir in the heavy cream, adding it 1 tablespoon at a time. Stir in the milk and salt.

2   In a small bowl, whisk together the cornstarch and eggs until the cornstarch is dissolved. Whisk the egg mixture into the butterscotch pudding mixture.

3   Cook over medium heat, stirring constantly with a whisk, until the pudding comes to a boil. Reduce the heat to a simmer, continue to stir, and cook for 2 minutes.

4   Pour the pudding into a container and stir in the whiskey and vanilla. Cover and refrigerate until thoroughly chilled.

5   **To caramelize the bananas:** Melt the butter in a large skillet with the vanilla bean. Stir in the brown sugar, add the banana slices, and cook over medium-high heat, without stirring, until the bananas begin to sizzle.

6   Add the coffee and continue to cook until the juices thicken to the consistency of maple syrup. Avoid stirring the bananas. Instead, tilt the pan and spoon the sauce over the bananas as they cook.

Serving: Dish up the pudding in individual custard cups or in tall glasses with the banana slices heaped over it.

BANANA CAKE WITH MOCHA ICING AND COFFEE CRUNCHIES

THE BANANA CAKE:

½ pound (2 sticks) unsalted butter, at room temperature

1½ cups sugar

1 teaspoon vanilla extract

1 tablespoon instant espresso powder

2 large eggs, at room temperature

2½ cups flour

1½ teaspoons baking powder

¾ teaspoon baking soda

½ teaspoon salt

1½ teaspoons ground cinnamon

6 tablespoons buttermilk, plain yogurt, or sour cream

2 cups banana purée (3 to 4 very ripe bananas)

1¼ cups pecans or walnuts, toasted and coarsely chopped

THE MOCHA ICING:

10 ounces bittersweet or semisweet chocolate, coarsely chopped

½ cup water or dark coffee

10 tablespoons (1¼ sticks) unsalted butter, at room temperature

Coffee and bananas a funny combination, you say? I say, get over it! After all, they're foods of the tropics. Coffee and bananas are wonderful together, and once you try this handsome stunner, you'll agree with me.

1   To make the cake: Position an oven rack in the center of the oven and preheat the oven to 350 degrees. Butter two 9-inch round cake pans, or line them with circles of parchment paper.

2   With an electric mixer or by hand, beat the butter and sugar for 3 to 5 minutes, until light and fluffy. Add the vanilla and the espresso powder, then beat in the eggs, stopping the mixer once or twice to scrape down the sides of the bowl.

3   Sift together the flour, baking powder, baking soda, salt, and cinnamon. Add half of the dry ingredients to the creamed butter mixture, then mix in the buttermilk and the banana purée. Mix in the remaining dry ingredients. Finally, add the nuts, stirring until completely mixed in, but don't overbeat.

4   Divide the batter between the 2 prepared pans and bake for 40 minutes, until golden brown and a toothpick inserted into the center comes out clean. Remove from the oven and allow to cool completely in pans.

5   To make the mocha icing: Measure the chocolate and water or coffee into a heatproof mixing bowl set over simmering water. Stir gently until the chocolate is melted. Cut the butter into 1-inch cubes and whisk them into the chocolate, whisking until the icing is smooth. Let cool to room temperature.

1½ cups sugar

¼ cup strong dark coffee

¼ cup light corn syrup

2 teaspoons vinegar

1 tablespoon baking soda,
sifted to remove lumps

6   Remove 1 cake layer from its pan and set it on a cake plate. Spread about ⅔ cup of the mocha icing over the top. Remove the other cake layer from its pan and place it over the iced layer. Spread the remaining icing evenly over the top and sides of the cake (see Note).

7   **To make the coffee crunchies:** Have an ungreased baking sheet handy.

8   Measure the sugar, coffee, corn syrup, and vinegar into a medium-size nonreactive saucepan with a capacity of at least 6 quarts. Fit a candy thermometer onto the side of the pan, and heat the liquid to 300 degrees. (You may need to tilt the pan to submerge the bulb of the thermometer for an accurate reading.) Remove from the heat and quickly stir in the baking soda with a wooden spoon. The mixture will foam, then start to thicken.

9   Immediately pour the mixture onto the baking sheet, before it hardens into a solid mass; do not spread. Let cool completely.

10   When completely cool, remove the mass from the baking sheet and chop into rough ½-inch pieces. Scatter the crunchies all over and around the cake.

Note: When icing a cake, pro icers like to spread a thin layer of icing over the top and sides and then refrigerate the cake for a few minutes until the layer of icing is firm. This makes the remaining icing easier to apply, resulting in a nicer finish.

MANGO AND LILIKOI BUTTER

ABOUT 3 CUPS

1 large mango (about
1 pound)

⅔ cup fresh or frozen
lilikoi (passion fruit) pulp

1 cup sugar

4 tablespoons (½ stick)
butter, salted or unsalted,
cut into small pieces

3 large eggs

1 large egg yolk

This recipe was adapted from one that Kelley Heldt generously shared with me. I worked with Kelley before he gave up his career as an aspiring chef to start a business in Hawaii called the Ko'olau Condiment Company. (He rejected the suggestion that he name it Kelley's Jellies.)

Lilikoi is both the Hawaiian word for passion fruit and the name of the district in east Maui where they are grown. Mango and lilikoi butter is undoubtedly Kelley's most popular condiment. It is delicious over fresh blackberries, spooned into cream puffs, or, as Kelley likes it best, served as a tangy accompaniment to a slice of dark, rich chocolate cake.

This is yummy, and best when made at least a day in advance to give it time to thicken.

1   Peel the mango and cut the flesh away from the pit. Cut the mango flesh into ½-inch pieces and purée in a food processor until very smooth.

2   In a medium-size nonreactive saucepan, whisk together the mango purée, lilikoi pulp, sugar, and butter.

3   In a separate bowl, whisk together the eggs and egg yolk. Whisk the egg mixture into the mango-lilikoi mixture.

4   Set a strainer—not too fine—over a heatproof mixing bowl.

5   Put the saucepan over medium heat and whisk until the mixture thickens and just begins to simmer, about 5 minutes. Immediately remove from the heat and pass the mango and

lilikoi butter through the strainer into the mixing bowl. Stir a few times to cool it down a little and refrigerate, uncovered, until cool. Once cool, cover it with plastic wrap and keep refrigerated for up to 1 week until serving.

Note: To juice fresh passion fruit, split passion fruit in half crosswise. Set a nonreactive strainer over a bowl and spoon pulp and seeds into the strainer. Use a flexible rubber spatula or spoon to press the pulp through the strainer. Discard the seeds, or do as I do, and mix a few into the finished passion fruit butter.

Grate a little lemon peel; can you smell the sudden squirting mist of lemon oil? Squeeze a plump tangerine; can you almost taste the sweet-tart juices before they start dripping? Slice into a blood orange; is there anything more beautiful than that sparkling multicolored cross section? The marvelous sweet-popping textures, the sunny intense colors, those unmistakable flavors—I don't think I could bake without the tangy juice and spritzy zest of citrus fruits.

CITRUS FRUITS

ORANGE-HONEY FRUIT SALAD WITH BOSTOCK

4 SERVINGS

THE FRUIT SALAD:

1 cup orange or tangerine juice, freshly squeezed (about 3 oranges or 4 tangerines)

¼ cup honey

1 cinnamon stick or ½ vanilla bean, split lengthwise

6 prunes, pitted and quartered

½ cup mixed dark and light raisins

2 cups fresh fruit (any combination of mango pieces, kiwi slices, seeded grape halves, banana slices, pineapple chunks, and navel or blood orange or grapefruit segments)

THE BOSTOCK:

1½ tablespoons plus 3 tablespoons sugar

3 tablespoons water

1 tablespoon rum, kirsch, or Grand Marnier

Optional: A few drops of orange-flower water

6 ounces almond paste (a generous ½ cup)

2 large eggs

Six ½-inch-thick slices of firm-textured white bread or brioche

½ to ¾ cup sliced almonds

Bostock may sound like a Swiss bouillon mix, but it's actually the word used by French pastry chefs to mean thick slices of good bread or brioche brushed with syrup and baked with a thick topping of frangipane. It's a fine, rich accompaniment to fruit salads like this one. Another worthwhile accompaniment would be the caramelized brioche (page 194). And don't forget how good a citrus fruit salad can be with a scoop of a tropical fruit-flavored ice cream or sorbet or with the blood orange sorbet on page 84.

1   **To make the fruit salad:** In a small saucepan, mix about ⅓ cup of the orange juice with the honey, cinnamon stick or vanilla bean, prune pieces, and raisins. Heat until the honey is dissolved. Remove from the heat and stir in the remaining orange juice.

2   Mix the fresh fruits in a bowl and pour the orange-honey syrup and the plumped dried fruits over them. Refrigerate for at least 1 hour, until thoroughly chilled. This fruit salad can be made up to 1 day in advance.

3   Position an oven rack in the top third of the oven and preheat the oven to 425 degrees.

4   **To make the bostock:** Measure 1½ tablespoons sugar, the water, and liquor into a small saucepan and heat until the sugar is dissolved. Add orange-flower water, if using. Set the syrup aside.

5   Beat the almond paste with the eggs and the remaining 3 tablespoons sugar until smooth.

6   Lay the bread or brioche slices on a baking sheet and brush them generously with the syrup. Spread the almond-paste topping on the slices, all the way to the edges, using all the topping (it will seem like a lot). Sprinkle the sliced almonds over the topping.

7   Bake the slices for 10 to 12 minutes, until the topping is crusty and golden brown. Serve wedges of bostock, warm or at room temperature, alongside bowls of the fruit salad.

BLOOD ORANGE SOUP WITH FROZEN RIESLING SABAYON

4 SERVINGS

THE FROZEN RIESLING SABAYON: (makes 1 quart)

4 large egg yolks

¾ cup sweet Riesling wine (or another white dessert wine)

½ cup sugar

1 cup heavy cream, softly whipped

A few drops of fresh lemon juice

THE BLOOD ORANGE SOUP:

1 cup fresh orange juice (about 3 oranges)

2 tablespoons sugar, or to taste

2 teaspoons light rum

3 blood oranges, peeled

1 navel orange, peeled

6 to 8 fresh mint leaves

The blood orange soup should be made fresh and served the same day. The sabayon will keep in the freezer for a week—a good thing, too, because this recipe makes more sabayon than you will need for four servings of blood orange soup. But I find it actually easier to whisk a sabayon with four egg yolks than with two.

1   **To make the sabayon:** Whisk together the egg yolks, wine, and sugar in a large heatproof bowl. Set the bowl over a saucepan of simmering water and whisk vigorously. The mixture will become first frothy, then thick and creamy. When it reaches the point where it holds a droopy shape when you lift the whisk, remove the bowl from the heat and whisk gently for 1 minute.

2   Fold in the whipped cream and the lemon juice. Transfer the mixture to a container and freeze, covered, for at least 8 hours.

3   **To make the soup:** Measure ¼ cup of the orange juice into a saucepan, add the sugar, and heat until the sugar is dissolved. Stir the sweetened juice back into the remaining ¾ cup orange juice, add the rum, and chill thoroughly.

4   To serve, either slice or segment the oranges and divide among 4 shallow bowls. Pour ¼ cup of the soup base over each serving. Finely chop or tear the mint leaves and scatter over the oranges. Add a creamy scoop of the frozen sabayon to each bowl, and serve.

Note: You can add some sliced fresh pineapple, sliced kumquats, or any flavorful berries to the soup.

BLOOD ORANGE SORBET SURPRISE

THE SORBET:
(about 3 cups)

2½ cups blood orange juice (about 4 pounds oranges, juiced, halves reserved)

10 tablespoons sugar

1 to 2 teaspoons Grand Marnier

THE MERINGUE:

3 large egg whites

½ cup sugar

½ teaspoon vanilla extract

Optional: A pinch of cream of tartar

If I reveal the surprise, promise you'll make this. The surprise is that the blood orange sorbet, nesting neatly inside orange cups, is concealed beneath a layer of airy meringue. Everyone who tested recipes for this book wanted to make this recipe first!

1   **To make the sorbet:** Warm ½ cup of the orange juice and the sugar in a small saucepan until the sugar is dissolved.

2   Stir in the remaining 2 cups orange juice and the Grand Marnier.

3   Chill thoroughly, then freeze in your ice cream maker according to the manufacturer's instructions.

4   Scrape out the reserved orange halves with a spoon, removing the pithy membranes and any remnants of pulp. The orange halves will serve as little sorbet cups. Slice a small piece off the base of each half if necessary to prevent it from wobbling.

5   Spoon freshly frozen sorbet into the 8 most presentable reserved orange shells, leaving about ½ inch of space for the meringue. Place the filled orange shells in a baking pan and chill in the freezer until firm.

6   Position an oven rack in the center of the oven, and preheat the oven to 450 degrees.

7   **To make the meringue:** Beat the egg whites either by hand or with an electric mixer until frothy. Add the cream of tartar, if using. Once the egg whites just begin to hold their shape, gradually sprinkle in the sugar and keep beating until they are stiff and shiny. Whisk in the vanilla.

8   Pile meringue into each of the sorbet-filled oranges and bake for about 5 minutes, until nicely brown. Serve immediately. (Once topped with meringue, the oranges can be kept in the freezer for up to 8 hours before baking.)

TOTALLY ORANGE ALLSPICE CAKE WITH BROWN SUGAR GLAZE

I wanted to make a cake that would be very orangey, but not too buttery, a cake that would resemble a *sformato,* the unmolded Italian pudding-soufflé. An idea from Giuliano Bugialli provided the jumping-off point, and here is the result.

THE CAKE:

1 medium navel orange (about ½ pound)

¼ teaspoon plus ½ teaspoon salt

1⅓ cups flour

½ teaspoon baking powder

½ teaspoon baking soda

2 teaspoons ground allspice

8 tablespoons (1 stick) unsalted butter, at room temperature

1½ cups granulated sugar

2 large eggs, at room temperature

1 teaspoon vanilla extract

½ cup milk

¾ cup currants, tossed in 1 tablespoon flour

THE GLAZE:

2 tablespoons unsalted butter

⅓ cup firmly packed dark brown sugar

3 tablespoons heavy cream

⅛ teaspoon salt

¼ teaspoon vanilla extract

1   **To make the cake:** Slice the orange in half and put it into a small saucepan. Add enough water to cover completely and ¼ teaspoon salt. Bring to a boil, reduce the heat to low, cover, and cook until the orange is limp, 1 to 1½ hours. (You should be able to pierce it easily with a sharp knife.) You can also cook the orange halves in a microwave oven on high power for 12 minutes. Finely chop the orange in a food processor (but do not purée) and set aside.

2   Position the oven rack in the center of the oven and preheat the oven to 350 degrees. Butter a 9 by 2-inch round cake pan.

3   Sift together the flour, the remaining ½ teaspoon salt, baking powder, baking soda, and allspice.

4   In a standing electric mixer, or by hand, beat together the 8 tablespoons of butter and granulated sugar until creamy and smooth, about 3 minutes.

5   Add the eggs and vanilla and continue to beat. Mix in half of the dry ingredients, the milk, and chopped orange. Stir in the remaining dry ingredients and the currants.

6   Transfer the batter to the prepared cake pan and bake for 50 minutes, until it feels slightly firm in the center. Cool before glazing.

7   Remove the cake from the pan and set it on a platter or cooling rack.

8   **To make the glaze:** Melt the 2 tablespoons of butter in a small saucepan. Stir in the brown sugar, and cook for 2 minutes, without stirring. Add the cream and salt and cook for another 2 minutes, stirring constantly. Remove from the heat and stir in the vanilla. Let the glaze cool for a few minutes.

9   When the glaze has cooled to lukewarm and has thickened somewhat, pour it onto the center of the cake and spread it to the edges with a butter knife or icing spatula, encouraging some of the glaze to drip down the sides.

RICOTTA CAKE WITH CANDIED ORANGE
AND ROSY RHUBARB SAUCE

ONE 9-INCH CAKE, 10 TO 12 SERVINGS

FOR THE CAKE:

2 pounds ricotta cheese
(whole milk or part-skim)

⅔ cup sugar

¼ cup heavy cream

5 large eggs, at room
temperature

1 tablespoon flour

1 teaspoon vanilla extract

½ cup golden raisins,
soaked in 3 tablespoons
warm Marsala or port

¾ teaspoon anise seed,
crushed

Grated zest of 1 orange

**THE QUICK-CANDIED
ORANGE PEEL:**

2 oranges, preferably
organic

1½ cups water

1½ cups sugar

**THE ROSY RHUBARB
SAUCE:** (makes 2 cups)

2 stalks (12 ounces)
rhubarb, trimmed of
leaves and root end

1½ cups water

3 to 4 tablespoons sugar

2 tablespoons Grand
Marnier

Although many people prefer ricotta cakes served warm, I prefer them chilled, like their American cheesecake cousins. Baker Nick Malgieri advises that overbaking a ricotta cake will cause it to release too much water. He also recommends that if your ricotta is grainy, you can force it through a coarse strainer to make it smoother.

The rosy rhubarb sauce here is worth trying with a simple baked apple or with the spiced apple charlotte on page 28.

1   Position the oven rack in the center of the oven and preheat the oven to 350 degrees. Butter a 9-inch springform pan.

2   **To make the cake:** Mix together the ricotta, ⅔ cup sugar, and heavy cream. Stir in the eggs, one at a time. Thoroughly mix in the flour, vanilla, raisins (and any remaining soaking liquid), the anise seed, and orange zest.

3   Transfer the batter to the prepared springform pan and bake for 1 hour, until golden brown.

4   **To quick-candy the orange peel:** Wash and peel the oranges with a vegetable peeler, removing 1-inch-wide strips of orange zest and none of the bitter white beneath. Cover the peels with water in a small saucepan. Bring to a boil and cook for 5 minutes. Drain off the water, and add the 1½ cups of water and 1½ cups of sugar to the pan. Cook over medium heat for 10 to 15 minutes, until the liquid has thickened and the peel is translucent. Drain through a strainer and discard the liquid.

5   **To make the rhubarb sauce:** Wash and dry the rhubarb. Slice the stalks lengthwise, then cut the rhubarb into ½-inch pieces. Simmer the rhubarb in the water in a medium saucepan for about 10 minutes, until tender.

6   Purée the rhubarb with the cooking liquid and 3 tablespoons sugar in a food processor. Taste and add more sugar if necessary. When cool, transfer to a bowl and stir in the Grand Marnier.

Serving: Once cake is chilled, remove from springform pan. Serve a slice of cake with the rhubarb sauce and candied orange strips alongside.

ANISE-ORANGE ICE CREAM PROFITEROLES
WITH CHOCOLATE SAUCE

I love the unorthodox combination of aromatic anise seed and dark chocolate. Who would have guessed it would make such a happy match?

THE ANISE-ORANGE ICE CREAM: (makes about 1 quart)

1½ cups milk

1 cup plus ½ cup heavy cream

1 cup sugar

1½ teaspoons anise seed

Pinch of salt

Zest of 2 oranges

5 large egg yolks

THE CREAM PUFFS: (makes 25 to 30 profiteroles)

1½ cups water

¼ teaspoon salt

1½ tablespoons sugar

12 tablespoons (1½ sticks) unsalted butter, cut into ½-inch cubes

1½ cups flour

5 large eggs

THE CHOCOLATE SAUCE: (makes 2 cups)

12 ounces bittersweet or semisweet chocolate

¾ cup water

¾ cup heavy cream

2 teaspoons whiskey, rum, or cognac

1   **To make the ice cream:** Warm the milk in a medium-size saucepan with ½ cup of the heavy cream and the sugar.

2   Grind the anise seed in a mortar and pestle or in a spice grinder, or crush them in a plastic freezer bag with a hammer. Add the anise seed, salt, and the orange zest to the warm milk. When the mixture is warm and begins to steam, remove from the heat, cover, and let stand for at least 1 hour to allow the flavors to infuse.

3   Stir together the egg yolks in a small bowl. Gradually add some of the infused milk, stirring constantly as you pour. Pour the warmed yolks from the bowl into the saucepan.

4   Cook over low heat, stirring and scraping the bottom constantly with a heat-resistant spatula, until the custard thickens enough to coat the spatula. Strain the custard into the remaining 1 cup of heavy cream. Discard the seeds and zest left behind in the strainer. Chill the custard thoroughly, then freeze in an ice cream maker according to the manufacturer's instructions.

5   Position the oven rack in the center of the oven and preheat the oven to 425 degrees. Line baking sheets with parchment paper.

6   **To make the cream puffs:** Bring the water, salt, sugar, and butter to the boil in a large heavy saucepan over medium heat, stirring frequently.

7   When the mixture begins to boil, add the flour all at once and stir continuously with a wooden spoon until the paste forms a ball and comes away from the sides of the pan.

8   Remove from the heat. Wait a minute, then begin beating the mixture, either by hand or in a standing electric mixer with a paddle attachment. Beat in the 4 eggs, one at a time, making sure each one is fully incorporated before adding the next. (I break the eggs into a bowl first to make sure no eggshell gets into the dough.) The dough (called *pâte à choux*) should be stiff and shiny.

9   Fill a pastry bag fitted with a ½-inch plain tip with the dough and pipe the dough onto the prepared sheets (or drop by spoonfuls) in 1½-inch-high mounds, at 3-inch intervals. When piping out this dough, the action of lifting the pastry bag often leaves a little point on each unbaked puff. To prevent them from burning, flatten any points with a dampened finger. Put the baking sheets in the oven and lower the heat to 375 degrees.

10   Bake the profiteroles for 25 to 30 minutes, until they are golden brown, both on top and up the sides. (If they are not fully cooked, they will collapse as they cool.) Remove them from the oven and poke each one in the side with a knife to release steam, which will otherwise make them soggy. Cool. (Profiteroles are best stored at room temperature for no more than several hours. They won't be as good, but they can be frozen for a few weeks, defrosted, and warmed for a few minutes in a preheated 350-degree oven.)

11   **To make the chocolate sauce:** Chop the chocolate into ½-inch pieces. Put the chocolate pieces in a heatproof bowl. Add the water and cream.

12   Set the bowl over a saucepan of simmering water and heat, stirring gently, until the chocolate is melted and the sauce is smooth. Remove from the heat and stir in the liquor. Keep warm.

Serving: Split the profiteroles in half and fill each with a scoop of the anise-orange ice cream, replace the tops, and spoon warm chocolate sauce over them.

BUCKWHEAT CRÊPES WITH TANGERINE BUTTERSCOTCH SAUCE

TWENTY 8-INCH CRÊPES, 6 SERVINGS

An updated crêpes Suzette. Lots of fun and less stuffy than the original, because mine has butterscotch sauce.

THE CRÊPES:

2 cups whole milk

1 tablespoon granulated sugar

¼ teaspoon salt

3 tablespoons unsalted butter

½ cup buckwheat flour

¾ cup all-purpose flour

3 large eggs

2 tablespoons Grand Marnier or Triple Sec

Grated zest of 1 orange

THE TANGERINE BUTTERSCOTCH SAUCE:

8 tablespoons (1 stick) unsalted butter, cut into ½-inch pieces

2 cups firmly packed light brown sugar

⅔ cup heavy cream

¼ teaspoon salt

½ cup fresh tangerine juice (2 or 3 tangerines)

¼ cup Grand Marnier, or to taste

Grated zest of 1 tangerine

4 tangerines (or oranges), peeled and segmented

1   **To make the crêpes:** Warm the milk, granulated sugar, salt, and butter in a saucepan over low heat until the butter has melted.

2   Pour the milk mixture into a blender and add the buckwheat and all-purpose flours, the eggs, the Grand Marnier, and orange zest. Blend at low speed until thoroughly mixed.

3   Refrigerate the crêpe batter for at least 1 hour.

4   To cook the crêpes, let the batter return to room temperature. Use a seasoned crêpe pan or an 8-inch nonstick skillet that has been very lightly oiled. Put the pan over medium-high heat. When it is hot, whisk the batter and ladle a very scant ¼ cup of the batter into the pan. Quickly swirl the pan to spread the batter into an even layer covering the bottom of the pan, and return the pan to the heat. The crêpe batter should begin to cook immediately when it hits the pan. (If the pan is too cool, the crêpe will stick and be soggy; if it's too hot, the crêpe will cook faster than you can swirl the batter into an even layer.)

Cook the crêpe about 1 minute. As it is cooking, use a butter knife to loosen the browned edges of the crêpe to prevent them from burning.

5   When the surface of the crêpe is covered with small bubble holes, lift the edge of the crêpe with the butter knife. With your fingers, or a spatula, lift up the crêpe and flip it over. Cook the second side for 30 seconds or so, until it has browned.

THE GRAND MARNIER
BUTTER:

½ pound (2 sticks)
unsalted butter, at room
temperature

⅓ cup powdered sugar

Grated zest of 2 tanger-
ines

¼ cup Grand Marnier

Note: The crêpes will
keep for up to 3 days in
the refrigerator, or they
can be further wrapped in
a layer of foil and frozen
for up to 2 months. The
sauce can be covered and
refrigerated for 2 weeks.

6   Turn the finished crêpe onto a dinner plate and immediately add more of the batter to the pan to start the next
crêpe. Stir the batter between crêpes to keep it homogenous:
Otherwise, since flour tends to sink, the batter at the bottom
of the bowl will be too thick. Keep making crêpes until all the
batter has been used, stacking the crêpes on the plate as you
go. If not to be served within a few hours, wrap them in plastic wrap and refrigerate until ready to use.

7   **To make the butterscotch sauce:** Measure the butter,
brown sugar, cream, and salt into a large skillet. Bring to a boil,
and boil for 3 minutes, without stirring.

8   Remove from the heat, then stir in the tangerine juice,
Grand Marnier, zest, and tangerine segments.

9   **To make the Grand Marnier butter:** Cream together the
butter, powdered sugar, zest, and Grand Marnier.

10   To assemble the crêpes, spread about 2 teaspoons of the
Grand Marnier butter over one quarter of each crêpe. Fold the
crêpes in half, then fold them again.

11   Divide the sauce and tangerines between two large skillets. Add the crêpes in a single layer in the skillets and warm
them over moderate heat until the sauce bubbles and the
crêpes are warmed through. (Or warm them in 2 batches in one
skillet, using half of the sauce for each batch.)

JELLIED TANGERINE JUICE

4 SERVINGS

1 tablespoon unflavored gelatin

3 tablespoons cold water

⅓ cup sugar

3 cups strained fresh tangerine juice (about 12 tangerines)

Optional: Fresh lemon juice

1 pint-basket strawberries, hulled, sliced, and tossed in a small amount of sugar

Sugar, to taste

When I was making desserts at Chez Panisse and Alice's daughter Fanny was about six years old, she asked me one day, "How come you never make Jell-O?" This is close.

1   Chill 4 wineglasses.

2   In a heatproof bowl, sprinkle the gelatin over the cold water and allow to stand for 5 minutes.

3   In a small saucepan, heat the sugar with ½ cup of the tangerine juice, stirring constantly, just until the sugar is dissolved. Pour the mixture over the gelatin and stir until the gelatin is also dissolved.

4   Whisk the mixture into the remaining 2½ cups tangerine juice. Taste and adjust with lemon juice, if necessary. Transfer the mixture to a measuring cup or pitcher with a spout and divide among the 4 chilled glasses. Refrigerate until set, at least 4 hours.

5   Top each serving with sweetened sliced strawberries before serving well chilled.

CHOCOLATE-TANGERINE SORBET

ABOUT 1 QUART

6 ounces bittersweet or
semisweet chocolate

1½ cups water

10 tablespoons sugar

1½ cups tangerine juice
(about 6 tangerines),
preferably freshly
squeezed

Sublime and refreshing. This is a great and easy dessert, with the rich flavor of dark chocolate and the refreshing tang of tangerine juice.

1   Chop the chocolate into ½-inch pieces.

2   Bring the water and sugar to a boil in a medium-size saucepan, stirring until the sugar is dissolved. Remove from the heat, add the chopped chocolate, and whisk until the chocolate is melted. Stir in the tangerine juice.

3   Freeze the chocolate-juice mixture in your ice cream maker according to the manufacturer's instructions.

LIME MARSHMALLOW PIE

ONE 9-INCH PIE, ABOUT 8 SERVINGS

THE GRAHAM-CRACKER CRUST:

1¼ cups whole-wheat flour

¾ teaspoon ground cinnamon

½ teaspoon ground ginger

5 tablespoons unsalted butter, chilled

2½ tablespoons honey

2 tablespoons sugar

3 tablespoons unsalted butter, melted

THE LIME CURD FILLING: (makes about 1½ cups)

½ cup fresh lime juice (4 to 5 limes)

½ cup sugar

3 large eggs

2 large egg yolks

6 tablespoons (¾ stick) unsalted butter, cut into ½-inch pieces

Grated zest of 2 limes

My lime pie is quite different from the traditional Key lime pie, because it has a creamy homemade marshmallow topping—which I love! I've always believed that to a baker a good marshmallow is like a good truffle to a chef. Of course, you could top this pie with 2 cups of sweetened whipped cream, but I think you'll have a blast making your own marshmallows. And if you make your own graham crackers, too, you'll have a homemade pie as homemade as a pie can be.

By the way, did you know that graham crackers were invented in the nineteenth century by a minister named Sylvester Graham, to curb lascivious urges?

1   Position an oven rack in the center of the oven and preheat the oven to 375 degrees. Grease a baking sheet or line it with parchment paper.

2   First make a big graham cracker: Mix together the flour, cinnamon, and ginger. Cut the chilled butter into ½-inch pieces. Cut the butter pieces into the dry ingredients with a pastry blender or your fingers, until the butter is in small pieces the size of grains of rice.

3   Knead in the honey until the dough is smooth.

4   Pat the dough into a circle about ⅛ inch thick on the prepared baking sheet. Bake for 15 minutes. Cool completely, then crumble about three quarters of the cracker into a food processor and grind into 1½ cups fine crumbs. (Eat the remaining quarter.) Or, seal the cracker pieces in a plastic freezer bag and crush with a rolling pin.

1 envelope unflavored gelatin

¼ cup plus ⅓ cup cold water

⅓ cup light corn syrup

½ cup sugar

3 large egg whites

1 teaspoon vanilla extract

5   **To make the graham-cracker crust:** Mix together the graham-cracker crumbs, sugar, and melted butter. Butter a 9-inch pie plate and pat the moistened crumbs into the pie plate in an even layer on the bottom and halfway up the sides. Bake for 10 minutes, then set aside to cool.

6   **To make the lime curd filling:** Whisk together the lime juice, sugar, eggs, egg yolks, butter, and zest in a medium-size nonreactive saucepan. Cook over medium heat, stirring constantly with a whisk, until the mixture thickens to the consistency of runny mayonnaise. Pour the filling through a coarse strainer into the baked crust. Bake the filled pie for 8 minutes, until the filling is just set. Remove the pie from the oven.

7   Reposition the oven rack in the upper third of the oven and increase the heat to 450 degrees.

8   **To make the marshmallow topping:** Sprinkle the gelatin over the ¼ cup cold water in a small bowl. In a small saucepan fitted with a candy thermometer, heat the remaining ⅓ cup water with the corn syrup and sugar. When the sugar syrup reaches about 210 degrees, start whipping the egg whites in a bowl with an electric mixer at medium speed. When the egg whites are frothy and the syrup temperature has climbed to 245 degrees, increase the mixer speed to high and slowly dribble the syrup into the whites as they are whipping, being careful to avoid pouring syrup on the beaters. (The beaters will fling off the hot syrup and it will stick to the sides of the bowl.)

9   Scrape the softened gelatin into the warm saucepan that was used to make the syrup, and stir until dissolved. Slowly

drizzle the gelatin into the whites as they are whipping. Add the vanilla and continue to beat for 5 to 10 minutes, until the mixture is white and fluffy, and has cooled to room temperature.

10   With a spatula, swirl the marshmallow topping over the entire top of the pie, making billowy peaks. Bake the pie for 4 minutes, until the top is deep golden brown. Remove to a wire rack.

Serving: Serve the pie at room temperature, or chilled. Use a sharp serrated knife dipped in warm water to slice the pie cleanly.

MARGARITA SORBET WITH CRISPY PEANUT COOKIES

THE SORBET:

½ cup granulated sugar

1½ cups water

Grated zest of 2 limes

½ cup fresh lime juice
(4 to 5 limes)

¼ cup tequila

4 teaspoons Triple Sec

THE COOKIES:

¾ cups unsalted roasted peanuts

¾ cup flour

8 tablespoons (1 stick) unsalted butter, at room temperature

½ cup granulated sugar

¼ cup firmly packed light brown sugar

1 large egg

1 teaspoon baking soda

2 teaspoons hot water

Coarse salt, for sprinkling

Serving: Serve individual scoops of the sorbet and pass a plate of the cookies.

This is a simple and singular combination of bracing Margarita sorbet and lightly salted peanut cookies. My inspiration was the firm disks of peanut paste available in Mexico. You won't believe how good this is until you're sitting outside in the hot sun with your own cool sorbet and crisp cookies.

1   **To make the sorbet:** Bring the granulated sugar and water to a boil in a saucepan. Remove from the heat and stir in the lime zest, lime juice, tequila, and Triple Sec. Chill the mixture thoroughly, then freeze in an ice cream maker according to the manufacturer's instructions.

2   **To make the cookies:** Grind the peanuts with the flour in a food processor until the nuts are in little pieces. (Or seal the peanuts in a plastic freezer bag and crush with a rolling pin.)

3   Beat together the butter and the granulated and light brown sugars in an electric mixer, or by hand, until just combined, about 30 seconds. Mix in the egg.

4   Mix the baking soda with the hot water and add to the batter. Mix in the ground peanuts and flour.

5   Position the oven rack in the center of the oven and preheat the oven to 325 degrees. Line a baking sheet with parchment paper.

6   Form the dough into 1-inch balls (a heaping teaspoon) and arrange them, at least 2½ inches apart, on the prepared baking sheet. Sprinkle each cookie with a generous pinch of coarse salt.

7   Bake the cookies for 8 to 9 minutes, until deep golden brown. Cool completely and store in an airtight container.

LIME CREAM PUFFS WITH SUGARED ALMONDS AND COCONUT-RUM "KAYA"

THE COCONUT-RUM "KAYA": (makes 2 cups)

¾ cup sugar

1¼ cups unsweetened coconut milk, warmed

2 tablespoons dark rum

Big pinch of salt

THE SUGARED ALMOND CREAM PUFFS:

25 to 30 unbaked cream puffs (page 90)

¾ cup sliced almonds

1 tablespoon light corn syrup

2½ teaspoons sugar

THE LIME CURD FILLING:

1½ cups lime curd (page 98)

⅓ cup heavy cream, whipped

True *kaya* is a Thai dessert made by cooking coconut milk for hours and hours. I make this quick version by caramelizing some sugar and adding coconut milk to stop the cooking.

Cram as many almonds as you can onto the unbaked cream puffs, since the cream puffs will expand a good amount during baking.

1   To make the coconut-rum "kaya": Spread the sugar in an even layer in a large nonreactive saucepan. Warm over moderate heat until the edges start to liquefy. Use a heatproof utensil to gently stir the melted sugar into the center to prevent it from burning too quickly. Continue to cook, stirring occasionally, until all the sugar is melted and has become a deep, rich brown color, like an old penny.

2   Remove from the heat and stir in half of the warm coconut milk. (You may want to wear an oven mitt, as the mixture will boil up vigorously.) Whisk in the remaining coconut milk, then stir the caramel over low heat to dissolve any lumps (stubborn lumps can be strained out before serving). Remove from the heat and stir in the rum and the salt.

3   To make the sugared almond cream puffs: Position the oven rack in the center of the oven and preheat the oven to 425 degrees. Have the cream puffs piped out on prepared baking sheets. Toss the sliced almonds in a bowl with the corn syrup and sugar. Press the sugared almonds onto the unbaked cream puffs. Bake according to the instructions in step 9 on page 40,

until the almonds are toasty brown. Remove from the oven and use a sharp paring knife to poke a hole in the side of each puff. Allow puffs to cool completely.

4   **To make the lime curd filling:** Fold together the chilled lime curd and the whipped cream.

Serving: Split the cream puffs and put the bottom halves on dessert plates, 2 or 3 per person, and spoon in 2 tablespoons of filling. Replace the tops and pour the "kaya" around them.

Variation: For a less rich dessert, instead of the "kaya," make a fresh mango sauce by puréeing a ripe mango with a few tablespoons of sugar and a shot of rum or a few drops of vanilla extract.

PINK GRAPEFRUIT CHAMPAGNE SORBET

I QUART SORBET, ENOUGH FOR AT LEAST 12 COCKTAILS

2 cups freshly squeezed pink grapefruit juice (3 pink grapefruits, about 3 pounds)

¾ cup sugar

I cup Champagne

The best reason for making pink grapefruit sorbet is so that you can enjoy the romance of concocting a truly unforgettable Champagne fruit cocktail. The recipe for the grapefruit sorbet is below, but you don't need a recipe for the cocktail. Just prepare some fruit: I suggest sections of grapefruit and oranges, quartered strawberries, and thin slices of kumquat—the quantities and proportions I leave entirely to you. Plop one or two scoops of the sorbet into well-chilled stemmed cocktail glasses. Add some fruit to each glass, fill almost to the brim with icy-cold Champagne, and serve.

I   Gently warm ½ cup of the grapefruit juice with the sugar in a nonreactive medium-size saucepan just long enough for the sugar to dissolve. Mix the sweetened juice with the remaining grapefruit juice and the Champagne.

2   Chill thoroughly, then freeze in your ice cream maker according to the manufacturer's instructions.

FREE-STYLE LEMON TARTLETS WITH WHITE CHOCOLATE SAUCE

6 TARTLETS

THE LEMON FILLING:
(makes 6 tartlets)

½ cup fresh lemon juice (about 3 lemons)

⅓ cup sugar

2 large eggs

2 large egg yolks

6 tablespoons butter, cut into ½-inch pieces

Grated zest of 2 lemons

THE TARTLET DOUGH:

1¼ cups flour

2 teaspoons sugar

½ teaspoon salt

5 tablespoons unsalted butter, chilled

4 tablespoons ice water

THE MERINGUE:

5 large egg whites

¼ teaspoon cream of tartar

Pinch of salt

10 tablespoons sugar

1 teaspoon vanilla extract

THE WHITE CHOCOLATE SAUCE:

3 ounces white chocolate

¼ cup half-and-half

Who would have thought that the contrast of smooth sweet white chocolate and sprightly lemon would work so fabulously well? I call these free-style tartlets because they're not baked in rigid tart pans—they're free-form. (You can also fill these delicious free-style tartlets with the Mango and Lilikoi Butter on page 76.)

1   **To make the lemon filling:** In a medium-size nonreactive saucepan, whisk together the lemon juice, sugar, eggs, egg yolks, butter, and zest. Cook the filling over medium heat, stirring constantly with a whisk, until the mixture thickens to the consistency of runny mayonnaise. Pour the filling through a coarse strainer into a container. Cover loosely and refrigerate.

2   **To make the tartlet dough:** Toss together the flour, sugar, and salt. Cut the butter into ¾-inch pieces and blend it in, using a standing electric mixer or a pastry blender, until the butter pieces are the size of corn kernels. Add the ice water and mix with your hand until the dough just begins to hold together. Form the dough into a 5-inch cylinder, wrap in plastic wrap, and refrigerate for at least 30 minutes.

3   To roll out the tartlet dough, slice the dough into 6 pieces. On a lightly floured surface, roll each circle of dough into a 5-inch disk. Stack the disks, separated by pieces of plastic wrap, on a plate, and refrigerate for 30 minutes.

4   To bake the dough, position the oven rack in the center of the oven and preheat the oven to 350 degrees. Place the disks of dough, evenly spaced, on a baking sheet and bake for 20 to 25 minutes, until golden brown. Cool completely.

5   To finish the tartlets, first place the oven rack in the upper third of the oven and increase the heat to 425 degrees.

6   Divide the lemon filling equally among the disks, mounding it in the center and leaving a 1-inch border all the way around.

7   **To make the meringue:** Beat the egg whites with an electric mixer until they become frothy. Add the cream of tartar and salt, increase the speed to medium-high, and continue to beat until they begin to form peaks. Gradually add the sugar, then the vanilla, and continue to beat until the meringue forms shiny, drooping peaks. Spoon the meringue decoratively over each tartlet, right to the edges, in dramatic swirling peaks. Return the tartlets to the oven and bake for about 5 minutes, until the meringue is golden brown.

8   **To make the white chocolate sauce:** Coarsely chop the white chocolate. Measure the half-and-half into a small saucepan, add the chopped white chocolate, and warm over low heat until the chocolate begins to melt. Remove from the heat and stir until the chocolate is completely melted.

Serving: Serve the tartlets with the warm white chocolate sauce drizzled around them.

Note: Lemon filling can be made up to 5 days in advance and refrigerated. Tartlet dough can be assembled and rolled up to 3 days ahead, but should be baked and served within a few hours of serving.

LEMON-GINGER CRÈME BRÛLÉE

6 SERVINGS

3 ounces fresh ginger, unpeeled and thinly sliced

3 cups half-and-half

½ cup plus 12 teaspoons sugar

Grated zest of 2 lemons

Pinch of salt

6 large egg yolks

Did you know that a *pot de crème* is just a *crème brûlée* without the burnt-sugar topping? Just about everyone seems to be wild about *crème brûlée*. You can even stock a purse-sized blowtorch to carry with you in case you need to perform an emergency operation on a *pot de crème*.

1   Put the ginger slices in a medium-size saucepan and add enough water to cover. Bring the water to a boil, reduce the heat, and simmer for 2 minutes. Drain the water, leaving the ginger in the pan.

2   Add the half-and-half, ½ cup sugar, lemon zest, and salt to the pan. Heat the mixture until it begins to steam. Remove from the heat, cover, and steep for 1 hour to infuse the liquid with flavor.

3   Position the oven rack in the center of the oven and preheat the oven to 350 degrees.

4   In a medium bowl, gently whisk the egg yolks until liquid. Rewarm the infused half-and-half mixture slightly. Pour a small amount of the infused half-and-half into the egg yolks, stirring constantly with the whisk.

5   Strain the infused cream mixture into a large measuring cup or pitcher and divide it among six 4- to 6-ounce ramekins or custard cups. Do not fill to the brims but leave ½ inch of room for the caramel layer. Put the ramekins or custard cups in a deep roasting pan and add warm water to the pan until it reaches halfway up the sides of the ramekins or cups. Cover the pan with foil and bake for 55 to 60 minutes, until the centers appear to be almost completely set.

6   Remove the custards from the water bath and set them on a wire rack to cool to room temperature.

7   Sprinkle each cooled custard with 2 teaspoons of sugar and caramelize with a blowtorch: Set the torch flame at medium, and wave the tip of the flame over the sugar at close range, until the sugar begins to melt. Rotate the ramekin with your other hand for even caramelization. Keep melting the sugar with the blowtorch until the sugar has darkened and caramelized. If you don't have a blowtorch, caramelize the sugar in a heavy pan on the stove over medium-high heat. When the sugar has reached a dark amber color, carefully pour it directly over each custard, lifting and tilting each ramekin while the caramel is still warm to distribute an even layer of caramel over the surface. Serve caramelized custards within 30 minutes.

Serving: Serve crème brûlée soon after the tops are caramelized, or within 30 minutes, to ensure a crispy, crackly topping.

LEMON QUARESIMALI

ABOUT 50 COOKIES

2 large eggs plus I egg, for brushing

I⅓ cups sugar

¾ teaspoon vanilla extract

Freshly grated zest of 2 lemons

I½ tablespoons fresh lemon juice

I¾ cups flour

I teaspoon baking soda

½ teaspoon salt

I½ teaspoons ground cinnamon

2 cups whole almonds, toasted

I usually call these Q cookies because it's easier for me to pronounce than their actual Italian name, *quaresimali*, which derives from *quaresima*, the forty days of Lent. These cookies deserve to be better known: They are firm and crispy and exceptionally good for dunking.

1   Preheat the oven to 350 degrees. Line 2 baking sheets with parchment paper.

2   In a medium-size bowl, whisk together the 2 eggs, sugar, vanilla, lemon zest, and lemon juice.

3   In a small bowl, mix together the flour, baking soda, salt, and cinnamon.

4   Stir the dry ingredients into the egg mixture until well blended, then mix in the whole almonds.

5   On one of the prepared baking sheets shape half the dough into a log about 13 inches long and 2½ inches in diameter. (I wet my hands to shape the dough.) Form the remaining dough into a similar log on the remaining baking sheet.

6   Stir the remaining egg in a small bowl and brush each log generously with egg wash. Once you've done this, do it again. (You won't use up all the egg.)

7   Bake the logs for 25 to 30 minutes, until golden brown and firm. For even baking, rotate the baking sheets and switch

racks after about 15 minutes. The logs will flatten out while baking. When done, remove the logs from the oven and reduce the heat to 300 degrees. Let the logs cool for 10 minutes.

8   With a sharp serrated bread knife, slice the logs cross-wise into 1-inch bars. Arrange the cookies, cut sides down, on the baking sheets and return to the oven for 20 minutes. Remove from the oven and cool completely. Store the cooled cookies in an airtight container for up to 1 week.

Variation: Substitute toasted hazelnuts, with loose skins removed, for the almonds.

SUPERLEMON SOUFFLÉ

6 INDIVIDUAL SOUFFLÉS

3 tablespoons flour

⅓ cup plus 1½ tablespoons sugar (plus additional sugar for coating the ramekins)

Pinch of salt

⅔ cup whole milk

4 large eggs, separated

2 tablespoons unsalted butter

3½ tablespoons freshly squeezed lemon juice

Grated zest of 1 lemon

¼ teaspoon cream of tartar

1 quick-candied lemon (page 114), chopped

FOR TOPPING THE SOUFFLÉS:

3 teaspoons sugar

1½ teaspoons freshly squeezed lemon juice

I think that the world is essentially divided into two types of people—lemon people and chocolate people. This recipe is for the lemon people.

1   Butter the insides of 6 individual 4-ounce ramekins or custard cups. Pour in some sugar and tilt the ramekins to coat the sides. Gently tap out any excess.

2   In a medium-size saucepan, whisk together the flour, ⅓ cup sugar, and salt. Whisk in one-third of the milk to make a smooth paste, then whisk in the remaining milk.

3   Set the saucepan over medium-high heat. Cook, stirring frequently, until the mixture thickens to a consistency of thin yogurt, about 5 minutes. Remove from the heat and whisk in the egg yolks and butter. Return the pan to the heat and cook until the mixture just begins to boil. You will see a few bubbles pop on the surface.

4   Transfer the mixture to a bowl that holds at least 4 quarts. Stir in the lemon zest and cool for 15 minutes. (The mixture can be made up to this point and refrigerated, well covered, for up to 3 days.) Stir in the fresh lemon juice.

5   To bake the soufflés, position the oven rack in the upper third of the oven (but not too close to the heating element) and preheat the oven to 400 degrees.

6   In another large bowl, whisk the egg whites until they are frothy. Add the cream of tartar and continue to whisk the egg whites until they begin to form soft, wet peaks. Whisk in

1 ½ tablespoons sugar. Beat until the peaks are stiff and shiny, but not dry. Fold one-fourth of the egg whites into the lemon soufflé base, then fold in the remaining whites along with the chopped candied lemon.

7   Fill each prepared ramekin to the top with the soufflé mixture. Sprinkle each with ½ teaspoon sugar and ¼ teaspoon fresh lemon juice. Then run your thumb around the inside perimeter of each ramekin, which helps the soufflés rise nicely.

8   Bake for 9 to 10 minutes, or until the tops are light brown and they quiver when nudged. Serve immediately.

Note: Depending on the size of your ramekins or custard cups, you may have a small amount of soufflé base left over. If so, bake it in another ramekin.

QUICK-CANDIED LEMONS

2 TO 3 LEMONS

2 to 3 lemons, preferably organic

2 cups sugar

1 cup water

I always candy a few lemons at a time. Although I use them in the previous recipe for Superlemon Soufflé, the chopped pieces are wonderful in place of the black-berries in the Gravenstein Apple and Blackberry Crisp (page 18) or simply draped next to your favorite lemon tart. Once Lindsey Shere, my pastry guru, gave me one precious bergamot, an uncommon citrus fruit, from her bergamot tree, and it candied beautifully. So feel free to substitute other citrus, such as oranges or tangerines.

1   Slice the lemons as thinly as possible. (I use a serrated steak knife.) Discard any seeds.

2   In a nonreactive saucepan, bring the sugar and water to a boil. Add the lemon slices and reduce the heat to a rolling simmer. Cook for about 30 minutes, until the slices are translucent.

Note: The candied slices can be kept in their syrup in a covered container, under refrigeration, for about 2 weeks. After that, they lose their appealing flavor.

GINGERY LEMONADE

2 to 3 ounces fresh ginger, unpeeled and cut into thin slices

3 cups water

½ cup sugar

1 cup strained freshly squeezed lemon juice (6 to 8 lemons)

Optional: ¼ to ½ cup cranberry or red grape juice

Great lemonade should be served outdoors, in tall glasses, poured over crackling ice cubes. Since I like ginger a lot, I use about 3 ounces per quart for a particularly robust lemonade. The more timid may prefer to make it with the smaller amount of ginger. Either way, pour it over plenty of ice in a tall glass. You can dress it up with a few slices of fresh lemon or turn it into pink lemonade by adding a small splash of red fruit juice—entirely suitable for a civilized croquet match or a deadly game of Jarts.

1   In a small saucepan, bring the ginger slices, water, and sugar to a boil.

2   Remove from the heat and cover. Let steep for 30 minutes.

3   Strain the sugar syrup into a pitcher and stir in the lemon juice and the cranberry or grape juice, if desired. Discard the ginger slices. Chill the lemonade thoroughly. Serve over lots of ice.

I have vivid early memories of the dried fruits my Syrian grandfather always fed me—in fact, my first fruit memory is of chewy dried apricots. He must have fed me dates, too, but the first date I can remember is still the best date I ever had: a creamy-smooth Medjool. Eating that delicious date consummated my love affair with dried fruits.

DRIED FRUITS

CHOCOLATE SOUFFLÉ CAKE WITH PRUNES, CRANBERRIES, AND KUMQUATS IN PORT

ONE 9-INCH CAKE, 10 TO 12 SERVINGS

THE CAKE:

12 (or 14) ounces bitter-sweet or semisweet chocolate

¼ cup coffee or water

¼ cup rum

¾ cup heavy cream

5 large eggs, at room temperature

½ cup sugar

THE FRUIT SAUCE:

2 cups Port

½ cup sugar

12 pitted prunes (dried plums), quartered

⅔ cup dried cranberries

12 kumquats, sliced and seeded

When I created this recipe, I made it over and over using different amounts of chocolate until I made it as chocolatey as I could. A friend I asked to sample the cakes looked at me and responded, "Too much chocolate? Is that possible?" So, if you love chocolate, feel free to use the additional 2 ounces of chocolate. And don't think your guests won't be happy to be offered a scoop of vanilla ice cream alongside.

1   Position the oven rack in the lower third of the oven and preheat the oven to 325 degrees. Butter a 9-inch springform pan. If it's not leakproof, put it on a large piece of aluminum foil and wrap the foil tightly around the outer sides. Set the springform pan in a larger pan with high sides, such as a roasting pan.

2   **To make the cake:** Coarsely chop the chocolate and place it in a large heatproof bowl. Add the coffee or water and rum and set the bowl over a saucepan of simmering water, stirring gently until the chocolate is melted and smooth. Remove from the heat.

3   Measure the heavy cream into the bowl of an electric mixer and beat until it forms soft creamy peaks. It should not be too stiff. Transfer the whipped cream to a separate bowl. Rinse and dry the mixer bowl.

4   Add the eggs and the sugar to the mixer bowl and whip at high speed until a ribbon is formed when you lift the beater, about 5 minutes.

5   Fold the eggs into the chocolate, then fold in the whipped cream.

6   Scrape the batter into the prepared springform pan. Then pour warm water into the larger pan until it reaches halfway up the sides of the cake pan.

7   Bake the cake for 45 minutes. It will feel soft in the center, but will firm up as it cools. Remove the cake from the water bath and cool on a wire rack for at least 1 hour.

8   **To make the fruit sauce:** Heat the Port and sugar in a small nonreactive saucepan. Add the prunes and cranberries and simmer for 4 minutes, until tender. Add the kumquats and simmer for 1 minute.

Serving: The best way to cut this exceptionally moist cake is to slice it with a length of dental floss pulled taut between your fingers. If you don't floss (which you should!), a sharp, thin knife will do nicely. Serve warm or at room temperature with the fruit sauce.

Variation: Blackberries in Port. 1 cup Port, $2/3$ cup sugar, 3 cups blackberries. Bring the Port and sugar to a boil in a small nonreactive saucepan. Cook for 3 minutes, add the blackberries, and cook gently until they just begin to soften. Serve at room temperature. (This sauce thickens nicely if made a day before serving.)

PEAR AND FIG CHUTNEY WITH BITTERSWEET CHOCOLATE MOUSSE

8 TO 10 SERVINGS

Chutney and mousse may sound like a surprising combination, but when you taste it, you won't be surprised: You'll be happy.

THE CHUTNEY:

10 dried pear halves (about 10 ounces), cut into ½-inch dice

¼ pound dried figs (8 to 12 figs), hard stems removed, cut into ¼-inch crescents

1 cinnamon stick

1 vanilla bean, split lengthwise

Four 1-inch strips lemon peel

⅔ cup light or dark brown sugar

Pinch of ground cloves

1 cup water

2 tablespoons apple cider vinegar

2 tablespoons whiskey or cognac

THE MOUSSE:

10 ounces bittersweet or semisweet chocolate

¾ cups whole milk

2 tablespoons sugar

4 large egg yolks

2 teaspoons rum or cognac

½ cup heavy cream

Serving: Serve the mousse in individual glasses with a big spoonful of the chutney on top.

1   To make the chutney: Put all the ingredients except the liquor in a medium-size saucepan. Bring to a boil, reduce the heat, and simmer until most of the liquid is absorbed, about 8 minutes. Remove from the heat and stir in the whiskey or cognac. Remove the vanilla bean and lemon peels. (The vanilla bean can be air-dried and reused.)

2   To make the mousse: Chop the chocolate into ½-inch chunks and put them in a large bowl. Set a mesh strainer over the bowl, or have one close at hand.

3   In a medium-size saucepan, warm the milk and the sugar. In a separate bowl, whisk the egg yolks until smooth. Slowly pour the warm milk mixture into the yolks, stirring constantly as you pour. Pour the mixture into the saucepan and cook over low heat, stirring constantly, until the custard begins to thicken and coats the spoon. Do not overcook or let boil.

4   Immediately pour the custard through the strainer into the chopped chocolate. Stir gently until the chocolate has melted and the mixture is smooth. Stir in the rum or cognac. Cool to room temperature.

5   Whip the heavy cream until it forms soft, droopy peaks. Do not overbeat. It should be loose and slide around when you move the bowl.

6   Fold one-third of the chocolate mixture into the whipped cream, then fold all the whipped cream back into the chocolate. Fold just until there are no streaks of cream visible. Cover and chill at least 2 hours before serving.

BRAZIL NUT, DATE, AND GINGER TART

ONE 9-INCH TART, 8 TO 10 SERVINGS

THE DOUGH:

4 tablespoons (½ stick) unsalted butter, at room temperature

¼ cup granulated sugar

1 large egg

1 cup flour

¼ teaspoon salt

THE FILLING:

1½ cups Brazil nuts

4 large egg yolks

1½ cups firmly packed light brown sugar

4 tablespoons (½ stick) unsalted butter, melted

1 tablespoon flour

¼ cup heavy cream (or milk)

¼ teaspoon salt

1½ tablespoons freshly grated ginger

12 large dates, pitted and cut into ½-inch pieces

I started using a lot of Brazil nuts years ago when I read that they were one of the few profitable crops that are friendly to the ecology of the South American rain forest.

The tart dough is a recipe from Gayle's Bakery in Capitola, a small northern California beach community that I love to visit. (Gayle Ortiz is not only the village baker's wife, she's now the village's mayor.) Gayle and her husband Joe Ortiz have written books about baking, horticulture, and golf.

Reserve a few scraps of dough in case the tart shell develops cracks while baking. It's easy to smooth over any fissures with a small piece of soft dough.

1   **To make the dough:** Beat the butter and granulated sugar in the bowl of an electric mixer, or by hand, for about 15 seconds, until just smooth.

2   Add the egg and continue to beat for 30 seconds, stopping the mixer to scrape down the sides. The mixture may look curdled.

3   Add the flour and salt and mix until the dough comes together. Form the dough into a disk, wrap in plastic wrap, and chill for at least 30 minutes.

4   On a lightly floured surface, roll out the dough, lifting it and sprinkling a little more flour on the surface to keep it from sticking, into a 12-inch circle.

5   Fold the circle of dough in half and transfer it to a 9-inch tart pan with a removable bottom. Center the dough in the pan, unfold it, and gently press it into the pan and up the sides. Roll

the rolling pin over the edge of the tart pan to shear off the excess dough; reserve the scraps. Freeze the tart shell for at least 30 minutes.

6   Position the oven rack in the center of the oven and preheat the oven to 375 degrees.

7   Prick the dough 6 times with a fork and bake for 20 to 25 minutes, until the tart shell is golden brown. (Check after a few minutes. If the sides have slipped, press them back up with your thumb.) Remove and cool completely. Reduce the oven to 350 degrees.

8   **To make the filling**: Toast the Brazil nuts for about 12 minutes, until they're golden brown and smell nutty. Coarsely chop them.

9   In a large bowl, whisk together the egg yolks, brown sugar, melted butter, flour, heavy cream, salt, and grated ginger until smooth. Mix in the date pieces and chopped Brazil nuts.

10   Pour the filling into the baked tart shell and bake the tart for 35 to 40 minutes, until the top is a uniformly deep brown and the filling doesn't jiggle when you shake it. Cool completely on a wire rack. Remove the sides of the tart pan before cutting and serving.

Note: The filling can be made up to 1 week in advance and refrigerated. Well wrapped, the dough can be kept in the refrigerator for 3 days, or frozen for 1 month.

Variation: For an even more tropically tinged dessert, for the brown sugar in the filling, substitute 1½ cups of palm sugar (available in Asian markets) and substitute coconut milk for the heavy cream.

SYRIAN-STYLE DATE-NUT TORTE

ONE 8-INCH CAKE, 8 TO 10 SERVINGS

12 ounces medium-size dates, pitted and quartered (about 2 cups pieces) (see Note)

1 cup walnuts, toasted and coarsely chopped

1 cup flour

1 teaspoon baking powder

¼ teaspoon salt

¾ teaspoon anise seed

3 large eggs

1 cup sugar

1 teaspoon vanilla extract

3 tablespoons orange juice

Powdered sugar, for dusting

Note: For a lighter version of this cake, use half the amount of dates—6 ounces, about 1 cup pieces.

My mother's ancestry was curious: Her forebears were Syrians and Danes. This is one of the few desserts that she made. The other kids would open their lunch boxes and find brownies or chocolate-chip cookies. I would open mine and pull out a neatly cut square of date-nut torte.

For historical accuracy, I recruited my Aunt Bunny to test my recipe against her memory. Bunny hopped into action, made the recipe, and insisted I add more dates than I thought altogether prudent. After taking her advice, I retested the recipe, and, lo and behold, Bunny knew best.

1   Position the oven rack in the center of the oven and preheat the oven to 350 degrees. Butter an 8-inch square cake pan and dust it with flour, tapping out any excess.

2   Use your fingers to toss and separate the date pieces and walnuts in a small bowl with a tablespoon of the flour.

3   In another bowl, mix the remaining flour with the baking powder and salt. Crush the anise seed in a mortar and pestle or seal them in a sturdy plastic bag and crush them with a hammer.

4   In a large bowl, mix together the eggs, sugar, vanilla, orange juice, and anise seed. Stir in the flour mixture, then the dates and nuts.

5   Transfer the batter to the prepared cake pan and bake for 40 minutes, until the top is light golden brown and the cake is just barely firm in the center. Cool completely, then dust heavily with powdered sugar. Cut into squares and serve. (Even though this cake has no butter in it, it can be enjoyed over the course of a few days.)

DATE, GINGER, AND CANDIED PINEAPPLE FRUITCAKE

TWO 9-INCH LOAVES

½ cup raisins

1 cup diced candied ginger (5 ounces)

1½ cups diced pitted dates (8 ounces)

1¾ cups diced candied pineapple (8 ounces)

Grated zest of 2 oranges

½ cup dark rum, plus at least ⅔ cup more for soaking the cakes

1½ cups macadamia nuts (or walnuts or pecans), toasted

1 cup shelled pistachios

2¾ cups flour

2 teaspoons baking powder

1 teaspoon freshly grated nutmeg

½ teaspoon salt

½ pound (2 sticks) unsalted butter, at room temperature

¾ cup sugar

3 tablespoons honey

6 large eggs, at room temperature

1 tablespoon vanilla extract

⅓ cup buttermilk or sour cream

One of my fruitcake secrets is to begin a day ahead, by dicing the candied fruit and soaking it overnight in rum. Feel free to change the proportions and types of candied fruits and nuts here to suit your taste. You can also substitute Grand Marnier or cognac for the rum. Michael, who photographed my desserts for this book, couldn't get enough of this cake. Neither could the rest of us in the studio, although there was serious competition from the Chocolate Cherry Fruitcake (page 132), shown alongside.

1   In a large bowl, toss the raisins, ginger, dates, pineapple, and orange zest together with the rum. Let stand overnight, tossing once or twice. (No, you don't have to wake up in the middle of the night. Do it before going to bed and when you get up in the morning.)

2   The next day, butter two 9 by 5-inch loaf pans that are at least 2½ inches deep. Cut a piece of parchment to fit in the bottom of each pan. Position the oven rack in the center of the oven and preheat the oven to 325 degrees.

3   Coarsely chop the macadamia nuts and add them to the bowl with the dried fruits. Stir in the pistachio nuts.

4   In another bowl, mix together the flour, baking powder, nutmeg, and salt.

5   In the bowl of an electric mixer, beat together the butter, sugar, and honey until smooth and creamy. Beat in the eggs, one at a time, scraping down the sides of the bowl as necessary. Add the vanilla. (The mixture will look curdled, which is fine.)

6   Mix in half of the dry ingredients, then the buttermilk or sour cream, and finally the remaining dry ingredients. Stir in the fruits and nuts.

7   Divide the batter equally between the prepared pans and bake for 55 minutes, until a toothpick inserted into the center comes out clean. When you remove the cakes from the oven, let them cool in the pans for 30 minutes, then pour about ⅓ cup of rum over each cake.

8   When they have cooled to room temperature, remove the cakes from the pans. Swaddle the cakes with pieces of rum-soaked cheesecloth and put them in plastic freezer bags. Keep in a cool place, bags slightly open. For the first week, drizzle in enough rum to moisten the cheesecloth every few days. After the first week, add more rum every few weeks.

Note: Once well soaked with rum, seal the bags. These cakes will keep at least a year. Mine are already a year and a half old. Some people prefer these freshly made, while others like them aged. The older they get, the mellower the flavors and the denser the texture.

PRUNE, COFFEE, CHOCOLATE, AND AMARETTO TIRAMISÙ

This was one of the first desserts that I made and served when I began working in the pastry department at Chez Panisse about twenty years ago. The chef at the time, Paul Bertolli, gave me a scrap of paper on which he had jotted down ideas for layers of a tiramisù. I had never even heard of such a dessert, and then, of course, I lost the piece of paper.

THE SPONGE CAKE:

6 large eggs, at room temperature

I cup sugar

I teaspoon vanilla extract

I cup flour

¼ teaspoon salt

THE PRUNE FILLING:

12 ounces pitted prunes (dried plums)

1¼ cups water

¼ cup sugar

¼ teaspoon almond extract

THE MASCARPONE CREAM:

2 cups mascarpone cheese

1½ cups heavy cream

½ cup sugar

THE COFFEE-AMARETTO SYRUP:

¾ cup espresso, or strong dark-brewed coffee

¾ cup amaretto

6 ounces bittersweet or semisweet chocolate, grated

Chocolate sauce (page 90)

1   Position the oven rack in the center of the oven and preheat the oven to 375 degrees.

2   **To make the sponge cake:** Beat the eggs in the bowl of an electric mixer with the sugar and vanilla for about 10 minutes, until a ribbon forms when you lift the whip. Meanwhile, lightly butter an 11 by 17-inch baking sheet. Either cover it with a sheet of parchment paper or dust it with a bit of flour and tap out any excess.

3   When a ribbon forms, remove the bowl of egg mixture from the mixer. Sift the flour and salt over the beaten eggs as you simultaneously fold them into the eggs, gently but thoroughly.

4   Spread the batter onto the prepared baking sheet and bake for 12 minutes, until the top is golden brown.

5   **To make the prune filling:** Heat the prunes, water, and sugar in a saucepan. Simmer the prunes gently for 10 minutes, then turn off the heat and let them cool in their syrup. Purée the prunes, their syrup, and the almond extract in a food processor. The purée should be as thick as soft peanut butter. Add a spoonful of water if necessary.

6   **To make the mascarpone cream:** In the bowl of an electric mixer, or by hand, whip the mascarpone and the heavy cream just until the mixture begins to mound and hold its shape; make sure it stays rather loose. Add the sugar and whip until soft and creamy, but not stiff. It should still slosh back and forth in the bowl if you rock it from side to side.

7   **To make the coffee-amaretto syrup and assemble the tiramisù:** Stir together the coffee and amaretto. Spread about 1 cup of the mascarpone cream in the bottom of a 2-quart baking dish. Sprinkle half the grated chocolate evenly over the cream. Cut a piece of sponge cake to fit snugly in the dish and place it over the grated chocolate. Slowly pour half of the coffee-amaretto syrup over the cake to soak it. Or brush it on the cake with a pastry brush.

Note: This is the ideal dessert for entertaining, since it is best assembled a day or two ahead. In fact, you can also bake the sponge cake in a 9 by 13-inch baking pan, until golden brown and springy in the center. Let cool, then remove from the baking pan and split horizontally. Assemble the tiramisù directly in the baking pan. Since the cake will be thicker, make the syrup with 1 cup each of espresso and amaretto.

8   Spread the prune filling over the soaked cake layer. Spread half the remaining mascarpone cream over the prune layer.

9   Cut another piece of cake to fit, place it in the dish on top of the mascarpone cream layer, and soak it with the remaining coffee-amaretto syrup. (Don't worry if it seems like a lot; it will all soak in.) Spread over the remaining mascarpone cream and sprinkle with the rest of the grated chocolate.

10   Cover with plastic wrap and refrigerate for at least 8 hours before serving.

Serving: Cut the tiramisù into squares. A good-sized spoonful of chocolate sauce should go with every serving.

PRUNE GÂTEAU BASQUE

ONE 9-INCH CAKE, 8 TO 10 SERVINGS

THE PRUNE FILLING:

8 ounces pitted prunes, quartered (about 1 cup)

3 tablespoons Armagnac or brandy

1 tablespoon rum

1 tablespoon anise-flavored liquor (such as ouzo, pastis, or anisette)

Grated zest of ½ orange

¼ cup sugar

¼ cup water

THE DOUGH:

1½ cups flour

½ cup sliced blanched almonds

1 teaspoon baking powder

¼ teaspoon salt

¾ cup sugar

8 tablespoons (1 stick) unsalted butter, at room temperature

1 large egg

1 large egg yolk

1 teaspoon vanilla extract

1 teaspoon almond extract

THE GLAZE:

1 large egg yolk

1 teaspoon milk or cream

This is easy: I make the dough in the food processor, scrape the processor bowl clean, and purée the prunes. My dried fruit adaptation is a little untraditional, but there is no definitive recipe for gâteau Basque. On a recent trip to southwestern France, I felt compelled to track down as many versions as I could find. None of them had prunes, although the prunes of the region are world-famous.

This dough is very soft and must be dusted with flour and rolled out between sheets of plastic wrap. Even then it may tear. The good news is that this dough is very forgiving and will bake beautifully regardless.

1   **To make the prune filling:** Heat the prunes in a saucepan with the Armagnac, rum, anise liquor, orange zest, sugar, and water. When the liquid comes to a boil, remove from the heat and let stand until the prunes are tender.

2   **To make the dough:** In the bowl of a food processor, process the flour, almonds, baking powder, and salt until the almonds are finely ground. Add the sugar and the butter and process until the butter is in tiny pieces. Add the egg, the egg yolk, and the almond and vanilla extracts and process until the dough is smooth.

3   Divide the dough into two pieces, one slightly larger than the other. Wrap each piece in plastic, shape into a disk, and refrigerate for at least 1 hour, until firm.

4   In the bowl of the food processor, pulse the prunes and their cooking liquid together until the mixture forms a slightly chunky purée.

5   Position the oven rack in the lower third of the oven and preheat the oven to 350 degrees. Butter a 9-inch springform pan, dust with flour, and tap out any excess.

6   To assemble the tart, remove one disk of dough from the refrigerator. Heavily dust both sides with flour, and roll out between 2 sheets of plastic wrap into a 10-inch circle. Remove the top sheet of plastic wrap and drape the dough, unwrapped side down, over the springform pan. Gently press the dough to fit into the bottom and partway up the sides of the pan. Peel the other piece of plastic away from the dough carefully to avoid tearing the dough. (If you do, dip your hand in flour and pinch any tears together.)

Variations: Gâteaux Basque are often filled with pastry cream or cherry jam. For a pastry cream gâteau, use about 1⅓ cups pastry cream flavored with 2 teaspoons rum, 1 teaspoon brandy, and ¾ teaspoon anise-flavored liquor.

For a cherry jam gâteau Basque, mix 1 cup of best-quality cherry jam or preserves with the same liquors as above. (Eastern European and Middle Eastern markets usually sell excellent sour cherry preserves.)

Glaze, bake, and cool both variations as directed for the prune gâteau.

7   Spread the prune filling over the dough in the springform pan, leaving a ½-inch border uncovered.

8   Dust the remaining disk of dough with flour and roll it out into a 9-inch circle between sheets of plastic wrap. Remove the top sheet, invert the circle of dough, and center it on top of the prune filling. Peel away the plastic wrap. Trim any excess dough from the bottom circle where it goes up the sides of the pan and fold the edge of that circle back over the upper piece of dough, pressing down gently to seal in the filling.

9   **To make the glaze:** Beat the egg yolk with the milk or cream and brush the top of the gâteau. Make a crosshatch pattern in the top by raking the dough with the tines of a fork.

10   Bake the tart for 40 minutes, until golden brown. Remove from the oven and cool completely before removing the sides of the springform pan and serving.

CHOCOLATE CHERRY FRUITCAKE

ONE BUNDT CAKE

My housepainter gave this cake a one-word review: "Awesome."

THE CAKE:

1½ cups dried cherries

¼ cup plus 6 tablespoons kirsch or rum

1 cup walnuts, pecans, or almonds, toasted

¾ cup bittersweet or semisweet chocolate chips

1¼ cups flour

½ cup unsweetened cocoa powder

½ teaspoon salt

½ teaspoon baking soda

½ teaspoon baking powder

10 tablespoons (1¼ sticks) unsalted butter, at room temperature

2 cups sugar

2 large eggs

1 large egg yolk

1 teaspoon vanilla extract

⅔ cup buttermilk or plain low-fat yogurt

1   To make the cake: Soak the dried cherries in the ¼ cup of kirsch or rum for at least 4 hours.

2   Position the oven rack in the center of the oven and preheat the oven to 350 degrees. Butter a 10-cup bundt or tube pan. Dust it with flour and tap out any excess.

3   Chop the nuts relatively fine, mix them with the chocolate chips, and set aside while you make the cake batter.

4   Sift together the flour, cocoa powder, salt, baking soda, and baking powder.

5   In the bowl of an electric mixer, or by hand, beat together the butter and the sugar until light and fluffy. In a small bowl, lightly mix together the eggs and the egg yolk. Slowly beat the egg mixture into the butter and sugar. Mix in the vanilla.

6   Stir in half the dry ingredients, then add the buttermilk or yogurt, and finally mix in the remaining dry ingredients. Gently stir in the nuts and chips.

7   Spoon the batter into the prepared cake pan and bake for 45 minutes. Remove from the oven and cool in the pan for 15 minutes. Poke 50 times with a toothpick, then slowly drizzle the remaining 6 tablespoons of kirsch or rum over the cake. Let cool 30 minutes, then invert the cake onto a large serving plate and cool completely.

2 tablespoons kirsch or light rum

I cup powdered sugar

8   **To glaze the cake:** Stir together the kirsch or rum and powdered sugar. Spoon the glaze over the top of the cake, allowing it to run freely down the sides.

Variations: For the cherries, substitute $1\frac{1}{2}$ cups Italian candied cherries or $1\frac{1}{2}$ cups of any diced dried fruit.

Instead of the powdered sugar glaze, drizzle the chocolate glaze on page 93 over the cake.

ABSOLUTE BEST BROWNIES WITH DRIED CHERRIES

9 TO 12 BROWNIES

6 tablespoons (¾ stick) butter, salted or unsalted

8 ounces bittersweet or semisweet chocolate

¾ cup sugar

1 teaspoon vanilla extract

2 large eggs

¼ cup flour

1 cup nuts, toasted and chopped (walnuts, almonds, hazelnuts, or pecans)

⅓ cup dried cherries, chopped

Optional: ⅓ cup Scharffen Berger Cocoa Nibs, see Note

I usually mistrust a recipe title with a superlative in it—"the ultimate" or "the world's very finest." Too often the results are less than wonderful. But what else can I call these brownies? I've finally worked out a perfect recipe for the absolute best brownie. And brownies are the perfect dessert. For one thing, the ingredients are easy to assemble. And this recipe is made in one saucepan, so there's very little cleanup. (I love that!)

This recipe has a distinguished lineage: It's my variation of a recipe adapted by chocolate expert Alice Medrich from a recipe by Robert Steinberg of Scharffen Berger Chocolate that began from a recipe by Maida Heatter. Please note, you *must* beat the batter for one minute before baking. The batter needs to be very smooth and velvety.

1   Preheat the oven to 350 degrees. Butter a 9-inch square cake pan and line the bottom with parchment paper.

2   Melt the butter in a medium-size saucepan. Chop the chocolate and add it into the butter, stirring over low heat until melted.

3   Remove from the heat and stir in the sugar and vanilla. Beat in the eggs, one at a time.

4   Add the flour and stir energetically for 1 minute, until the batter loses its graininess and becomes smooth and glossy.

5   Stir in the chopped nuts, cherries, and the cocoa nibs, if using. Scrape the batter into the prepared cake pan and bake for 30 minutes. Cool completely before removing the brownies from the pan.

Note: These brownies will keep well for up to 4 days at room temperature, and can be frozen for 6 months if well wrapped.

Variation: I once had what I thought was the perfect scheme for getting invited to appear on a very popular television program: I sent the host and her producers a batch of these brownies flavored with Altoid mints, which I knew the host loved. The day they arrived, I received an enthusiastic phone call raving about how much the star and her staff loved them, but I never heard from them after that. Her loss, your gain.

This was my ploy: Follow the recipe above, but omit the dried cherries. Crush the contents of one 50-gram tin of peppermint Altoids in a plastic freezer bag. Add the crushed mints to the brownies along with the nuts (or omit the nuts) and bake as directed.

Note: Cocoa nibs are available at www.scharffenberger.com, or 1-800-930-4528.

PISTACHIO, ALMOND, AND CHERRY BARK

ABOUT 1¼ POUNDS OF CANDY

20 ounces bittersweet or semisweet chocolate

½ cup whole almonds, toasted

¼ cup shelled pistachios

¼ cup dried cherries

"Tempering" chocolate is a process of manipulating the temperature of chocolate so that it hardens to be dark, smooth, and glossy, and so that no dull streaks of cocoa fat form on the surface. When I taught classes with John Scharffenberger, I showed him this simple method for tempering, and he claims it's the easiest ever.

Avoid allowing even a tiny amount of water anywhere near your silky-smooth melted chocolate and don't even try to temper chocolate if the weather is hot and humid. If you have melted chocolate over simmering water, when you remove the bowl, wipe the outside dry with a towel to avoid dripping water. I also strongly recommend using a digital or glass chocolate thermometer, because they are the most accurate. For how to order a chocolate thermometer, see the Note on page 137.

1   Chop 16 ounces of the chocolate. Put the chopped chocolate in a dry metal bowl and place it over a saucepan of simmering water. Stir frequently until the chocolate reaches a temperature of about 120 degrees on a digital or chocolate thermometer.

2   Remove the bowl from the simmering water, and set it on a dry folded towel. Add the remaining 4-ounce block of chocolate. Let stand, stirring occasionally, until the temperature has cooled to the low 80s.

3   Have the nuts and dried cherries ready nearby. Stretch a sheet of plastic wrap over a baking sheet (which will give the bark a shiny bottom), or line a baking pan with parchment paper.

4   Replace the bowl of chocolate over the saucepan of simmering water. "Flash" the bowl over the water for 3 to 5 seconds. Remove it, stir the chocolate, and replace the bowl, repeating the process until the temperature reads between 88 and 91 degrees. You'll probably need to flash the bowl several times to get the chocolate to the correct temperature. (Do not be tempted to keep it over the heat until it reaches the correct temperature, because the temperature will keep climbing once you remove the bowl, and if it goes over 92 degrees, you'll need to start all over again.)

5   Immediately stir in the nuts and cherries, then spread the mixture out on the prepared baking sheet. Place the baking sheet in a very cool, drafty place, or in the refrigerator, until the chocolate is set, 5 to 10 minutes. Break the bark into pieces to serve, or store in a cool place (but not the refrigerator) for up to 2 weeks.

Note: Chocolate thermometers can be ordered from Sweet Celebrations at www.sweetc.com, or 1-800-328-6722.

PEPPERY CHOCOLATE-CHERRY BISCOTTI

50 TO 60 COOKIES

¾ cup dried sour cherries

2 tablespoons kirsch
(or another liquor)

I cup almonds (or
hazelnuts)

2 cups flour

¾ cups unsweetened
Dutch-process cocoa
powder

I teaspoon baking soda

I teaspoon freshly ground
black pepper

¼ teaspoon salt

3 large eggs plus I egg
for egg wash

I cup sugar

½ teaspoon almond
extract

¾ cup semisweet
chocolate chips

2 tablespoons coarse
or granulated sugar

I'm nuts about biscotti. They're not supersweet and they go equally well with dessert wines and with coffee. I love them in the morning, but I could eat these all day. Which I do.

1   Coarsely chop the dried cherries and toss them with the kirsch in a bowl. Let steep for at least 1 hour.

2   Preheat the oven to 350 degrees. Line a baking sheet with parchment paper.

3   Spread the almonds or hazelnuts on a baking sheet and toast for 10 to 12 minutes. Remove from the oven and cool. Once they are cool, chop them very coarsely. (If using hazelnuts, remove any loose skin.)

4   Sift the flour, cocoa powder, baking soda, pepper, and salt into a large bowl.

5   In another bowl, beat together the 3 eggs, sugar, and almond extract. Gradually stir in the dry ingredients, then add the cherries and kirsch, the nuts, and the chocolate chips, mixing until the dough holds together.

6   Divide the dough in half. On a lightly floured surface, roll the dough into two 14-inch logs. Place the logs, spaced evenly apart, on the prepared baking sheet.

7   Gently flatten the tops of the logs. Beat the remaining egg and liberally brush the tops of the logs with it. (You will

have some left over.) Sprinkle the tops with the coarse or granulated sugar and bake for 25 minutes, until the logs feel firm to the touch.

8   Remove the baking sheet from the oven and cool for 15 minutes. Place the logs on a cutting board and with a serrated knife cut them diagonally into $\frac{1}{2}$-inch slices. Lay the cookies cut side down on baking sheets and bake for 20 minutes, rotating the baking sheets and switching racks midway through baking. Cool the cookies completely and store in an airtight container for up to 2 weeks.

APRICOT ICE CREAM TARTUFI

10 TO 12 SERVINGS

THE APRICOT ICE
CREAM: (makes 5 cups)

¾ cup dry white wine
(or orange juice)

1½ tablespoons plus
¾ cup sugar

6 ounces dried California
apricot halves (about
1½ cups), cut into small
pieces

1 cup milk

1 cup plus 1 cup heavy
cream

5 large egg yolks

A few drops of vanilla
or almond extract

1¼ pounds bittersweet or
semisweet chocolate

THE APRICOT SAUCE:
(makes 2½ cups)

2¼ cups orange juice

2 tablespoons sugar

3 ounces dried California
apricot halves (about ¼
cup), cut into small pieces

A few drops of vanilla
extract

⅓ cup chopped pistachio
nuts

A *tartufo* is actually meant to resemble a big ol' truffle. (*Tartufo* is Italian for truffle.) Forming ice cream into spheres, dipping them in melted chocolate, and sprinkling them with chopped pistachio nuts elevates ice cream into something more fun and interesting (and easy) than your usual fancy ice cream bombe, say.

It's vital to use California apricots in this recipe. The imported varieties (often from Turkey) are quite sweet and don't have the same tang and depth of flavor. Kitchen scissors work very well for snipping them into little pieces. When dipping the *tartufi*, be sure not to let any little pieces of ice cream fall into the chocolate, which can cause it to harden and seize.

1   **To make the ice cream:** Bring the wine and 1½ tablespoons sugar to a boil in a nonreactive medium-size saucepan. Add the apricot pieces, cover, and let stand until tender, about 15 minutes. Purée in a food processor or pass through a food mill. Set aside.

2   Warm the milk, 1 cup of heavy cream, and the ¾ cup sugar in another medium-size saucepan.

3   Pour the remaining 1 cup of heavy cream into a separate container and set a fine-mesh strainer over the container.

4   Whisk together the egg yolks in a bowl. Gradually pour in some of the warmed milk mixture, stirring constantly as you pour. Pour the warmed yolks back into the saucepan.

5   Cook over low heat, constantly stirring and scraping the bottom of the pan with a heat-resistant spatula, until the custard thickens enough to coat the spatula.

6   Strain the custard through the waiting strainer into the remaining 1 cup of heavy cream. Stir in the apricot purée and the vanilla or almond extract. Chill the mixture thoroughly, then freeze in an ice cream maker according to the manufacturer's instructions. (If the mixture is too thick, beat it with a whisk to thin it out.) After you remove the ice cream from the ice cream maker, store it in your freezer until firm, preferably overnight.

7   Cover two plates with plastic wrap. Using an ice cream scoop and your hands, form the ice cream into 10 to 12 smooth balls, each about 2 inches in diameter. (You may need to shuttle the ice cream back and forth from the freezer if it's a warm day—or if you're a slowpoke.) Set the ice cream balls on the plates and freeze thoroughly.

8   Chop the chocolate into ½-inch pieces and melt in a clean, dry bowl set over a saucepan of simmering water. Stir until melted.

9   Using two forks and working speedily, roll each ice cream ball in the melted chocolate until coated. As you lift each *tartufo* from the chocolate, scrape the bottom against the side of the bowl to remove the chocolate "foot." Place the *tartufi* in the freezer until ready to serve.

10   **To make the apricot sauce:** Warm the orange juice, sugar, and apricot pieces in a medium-size nonreactive saucepan. (Don't boil, or the juice will get bitter.) Remove from the heat, cover, and let stand 15 minutes. Purée in a blender or food processor. Add vanilla to taste.

Serving: Serve the *tartufi* with some of the apricot sauce and a sprinkling of crunchy pistachios.

APRICOT FILO TRIANGLES WITH RETSINA SYRUP

8 SERVINGS

THE FILO TRIANGLES:

4 ounces dried California apricot halves

¾ cup retsina wine, or dry white wine

2½ tablespoons sugar

3 ounces cream cheese, regular or reduced fat

½ teaspoon vanilla extract

8 sheets of filo dough

4 tablespoons (½ stick) unsalted butter, melted

THE RETSINA SYRUP:
(makes about 1¼ cups)

1⅓ cups retsina wine

¾ cup mild-flavored honey

⅛ teaspoon orange-flower water

I love Greece, but I haven't been able to get there since my backpacking collegiate travel days—which was quite a long time ago. But I do remember sunny days on beautiful Aegean beaches in various states of undress, and warm nights on the Plaka eating moussaka and filo pastries and washing it all down with surprisingly agreeable retsina, the resin-scented wine that's drunk at just about every opportunity in Greece. So occasionally, instead of booking passage to Greece, I'll enjoy a bottle of retsina at home, usually fully clothed.

When making the filo triangles, it helps to think about the dough in thirds—upper, middle, and lower. The middle third is where the filling is, and the upper and lower thirds are folded over it.

1   **To make the filo triangles:** In a small nonreactive saucepan, warm together the apricots and the ¾ cup retsina, cooking until the apricots have absorbed most of the wine. Cool.

2   With a fork or in a food processor, mash the apricots together with the sugar, cream cheese, and vanilla.

3   Position the oven rack in the center of the oven and preheat the oven to 375 degrees. Line a baking sheet with parchment paper or lightly butter it.

4   Unwrap the sheets of filo dough and lay them on the counter, covering them immediately with a damp kitchen towel. Remove 1 sheet of filo dough and re-cover the other

sheets with the towel. Place the sheet horizontally on your work surface. Spoon about 3 tablespoons of the apricot filling (an equal portion, see Note) at the far left of the filo sheet centered between the top and bottom. Brush the exposed dough with melted butter. (Working quickly is more important than brushing thoroughly here.)

5   Fold the upper third of the dough over the center section, then fold the lower third of the dough over the center. Brush the exposed dough with melted butter, and loosely fold the dough into a triangle, as if folding up a flag, enclosing the apricot filling. Repeat the process with the remaining filo sheets and the rest of the apricot filling.

6   Place the triangles on the prepared baking sheet, brush the tops with melted butter, and bake for 20 to 25 minutes, until golden brown. Some filling may ooze out during baking, which is fine.

7   **To make the retsina-honey syrup:** Bring the $1\frac{1}{3}$ cups retsina to a boil with the honey. When the honey is dissolved, reduce the heat to a low boil and cook for 5 minutes to thicken. Remove from the heat and stir in the orange-flower water.

Serving: Spoon the syrup generously around the warm filo triangles. If there is any left over, it is sensational spooned over sliced oranges or strawberries. The syrup will keep for 2 months, refrigerated.

Note: To divide the filling into 8 equal portions, spread it evenly onto a small plate and make indentations for 8 wedges, as if portioning a pie.

HAZELNUT, APRICOT, AND CHOCOLATE DACQUOISE WITH APRICOT SAUCE

6 INDIVIDUAL CAKES

THE MERINGUES:

¾ cup hazelnuts, toasted

1 cup finely diced dried California apricots (5 ounces)

¼ cup unsweetened Dutch-process cocoa powder

5 large egg whites

Pinch of salt

¾ cup sugar

2 tablespoons apricot jam (strained, if chunky)

½ teaspoon vanilla extract

THE FILLING:

8 ounces bittersweet or semisweet chocolate

6 tablespoons water

1 tablespoon Frangelico or cognac

¾ cup heavy cream

THE APRICOT SAUCE:

¾ cup apricot jam

6 tablespoons hot water

Fresh lemon juice, to taste

2 teaspoons Frangelico or Grand Marnier

This is the ultimate do-ahead dessert, since you absolutely must make it at least one day before serving, to allow the flavors to sublimely meld into each other overnight. I insist that you use tangy California apricots. The imported ones are just too damn sweet. These are rich little cakes, but your guests might still like some whipped cream alongside, or chocolate sauce (page 90), in addition to, or instead of, the apricot sauce. (The apricot sauce also goes well with the apricot filo triangles on page 142 and with the Brazil Nut, Date, and Ginger Tart on page 122.)

1   Preheat the oven to 275 degrees. Measure 2 sheets of parchment paper to fit 2 baking sheets. On each sheet of parchment paper, trace six 4-inch circles with a marking pen or pencil. (As a guide, use a round cookie cutter, a can with a 4-inch diameter, or a small plate.) Turn the sheets of paper over on the baking sheets so the unmarked side of the paper faces up. You will be able to see through the translucent paper and discern the circles marked on the other side.

2   **To make the meringues:** Rub the toasted hazelnuts in a kitchen towel to remove any loose skins. Chop the hazelnuts very coarsely (into halves, more or less). Toss the nuts in a small bowl with the diced apricots and cocoa powder, separating the sticky apricot pieces.

3   In a large metal bowl, or using an electric mixer, whip the egg whites with the salt until they begin to hold their shape when you lift the whip. Gradually whip in the sugar, a bit at a time, until the whites are thick and glossy, 2 to 3 minutes. Whip in the apricot jam and the vanilla. Use a rubber spatula to fold in the apricot and hazelnut mixture.

4   Divide the meringue evenly among the 12 circles on the parchment paper sheets, spreading each meringue disk into an even layer within the guide circle. Bake the meringues for 1 hour, then turn the oven off and leave the meringues in the oven an additional 30 minutes. Remove from the oven and cool completely on the baking sheets.

5   **To make the filling:** Coarsely chop the chocolate and put it in a heatproof bowl with the water and Frangelico or cognac. Set over a pan of simmering water and stir gently until the chocolate has melted. Remove from the heat and let cool to room temperature.

6   Whip the cream until it forms soft, droopy peaks. Fold the chocolate mixture into the whipped cream and chill for 30 minutes.

7   **To make the apricot sauce:** Stir together the apricot jam and the hot water until smooth. Add a few drops of lemon juice, to taste, and stir in the Frangelico or Grand Marnier. Feel free to include a swirl of chocolate sauce (page 90).

8   To assemble the individual dacquoises, carefully peel the meringue disks off the parchment paper. Divide the chocolate filling evenly among 6 of the disks, spreading an even layer on the smooth underside of each of the meringues (the "private side," as Julia Child calls it). Gently sandwich the filling with the remaining 6 meringues. Wrap in plastic and refrigerate for at least 24 hours, or up to 3 days. These can also be frozen, if well wrapped, for up to 3 months. Allow the cakes to come to room temperature, and serve with the apricot sauce.

Variation: Instead of the chocolate filling, sandwich apricot ice cream (page 140) between the meringues, or use any favorite frozen filling. Allow about ⅓ cup of filling per meringue.

CRANZAC COOKIES

ABOUT 26 COOKIES

1¼ cups flour

1 cup rolled oats

1 cup firmly packed light brown sugar

1 cup dried shredded coconut, sweetened or unsweetened

½ teaspoon baking soda

¼ teaspoon salt

½ cup dried cranberries

3 tablespoons water

4 tablespoons (½ stick) unsalted butter, melted

¼ cup Lyle's Golden Syrup (available in well-stocked supermarkets)

Anzac is an acronym for the Australian and New Zealand Army Corps—the down-under force that fought in World War I. The original Anzac cookie recipe was developed back then to provide the soldiers with a nutritious energy boost, the precursor to the ubiquitous energy bars. I've adapted a recipe that appeared in *Cooking Light* magazine and added dried cranberries.

1   Position the oven rack in the center of the oven and preheat the oven to 350 degrees. Line a baking sheet with parchment paper.

2   In a large bowl, toss together the flour, oats, brown sugar, coconut, baking soda, salt, and dried cranberries.

3   Stir in the water, melted butter, and Golden Syrup until the dry ingredients are thoroughly moistened.

4   Roll the cookie dough into 1¼-inch balls. Place the balls on the baking sheet, about 1 inch apart, and flatten them into 2-inch disks.

5   Bake the cookies for 12 minutes, until light brown. Rotate the baking sheet midway through baking to make sure the cookies bake evenly. Once cool, store the cookies in an airtight container for up to 3 days. The dough can be made in advance and refrigerated for up to 1 week or frozen for longer.

Variation: Substitute ½ cup raisins or dried cherries for the dried cranberries.

These are fruits I'm always in the mood for: cool, sweet orange and green crescents of melon, slippery with seeds; voluptuous bunches of just-washed grapes, bursting at the stems with sweet nectar; and syrupy fresh figs, so enticing in their moment of perfect ripeness, their skins splitting to reveal juicy flesh within.

FIGS, GRAPES, MELON, AND POMEGRANATES

FRESH FIG AND RASPBERRY TART WITH HONEY

ONE 9-INCH TART, 8 SERVINGS

THE TART DOUGH:

6 tablespoons (¾ stick) unsalted butter, chilled

½ cup sugar

2 large egg yolks

¾ teaspoon almond extract

½ cup sliced almonds, very finely ground

1 cup flour

½ teaspoon salt

THE FRUIT TOPPING:

¼ cup raspberry jam

10 to 12 medium-size ripe fresh figs

One 6-ounce basket raspberries

3 tablespoons honey

Optional: Mascarpone or whipped cream

The tart dough is sturdy enough to hold up all day without losing any of its crispiness and buttery-ness. For best results, grind the almonds in a food processor. Then you can make the dough in the food processor, too, without having to wash the bowl. You *could* strain the seeds out of the raspberry jam, but I like them. To me, the seeds are what raspberries are all about.

1   **To make the tart dough:** In the bowl of an electric mixer or food processor, or by hand, mix together the butter and sugar until no lumps of butter are visible. Beat in the egg yolks and almond extract. Add the ground almonds, flour, and salt and mix at low speed until the dough begins to come together.

2   Lightly butter the bottom and sides of a 9-inch tart pan. Gather the dough and press it evenly into the bottom of the pan and up the sides with the heel of your hand. (If it sticks to your hands, chill the dough briefly and dust your hands with a bit of flour.) Put the tart pan in the freezer for at least 30 minutes.

3   Position the oven rack in the center of the oven and preheat the oven to 375 degrees.

4   Prick the tart dough 10 times with a fork. Line the dough with a sheet of aluminum foil and cover with a layer of pie weights, dried beans, or raw rice. Bake for 20 minutes. Remove the foil and pie weights and bake an additional 5 to 10 minutes, until the tart shell is golden brown. Remove from the oven and cool.

5   **To assemble the tart and its fruit topping:** Spread the raspberry jam in an even layer over the tart shell. Quarter the figs, remove any hard stems, and arrange the quarters on the tart shell in two concentric circles, cut side up, fitting them snugly against the sides of the tart shell and each other. In the center, tightly arrange the raspberries.

6   Warm the honey and drizzle it over the tart.

Serving: Serve with a dollop of mascarpone or whipped cream if you wish.

Note: This tart is best the day it is assembled. The dough, however, can be frozen for up to 2 months if well wrapped.

HOMEMADE RICOTTA WITH FRESH FIGS AND CHESTNUT HONEY

4 SERVINGS

THE RICOTTA:

1 quart whole milk

½ cup plain whole-milk yogurt

Optional: ½ cup heavy cream

½ teaspoon salt

6 ripe fresh figs

2 teaspoons chestnut honey (or another strongly flavored honey)

It's great fun to make your own ricotta. Served with figs and honey, it makes a superb dessert with sherry—either dry or sweet. (It would also be good with the honey-poached pears on page 34 or the spice-baked pears on page 42.)

1   To make the ricotta: In a medium-size saucepan, bring the milk and yogurt (and heavy cream, if using) to a boil. Boil for 1 to 2 minutes, until the milk is curdled.

2   Remove from the heat. Line a strainer with cheesecloth and set it over a deep bowl. Pour the milk mixture into the strainer and let drain for 15 minutes. Gather the cheesecloth around the curds and squeeze gently to extract any excess liquid.

3   To serve the dessert, quarter or slice the figs. Scoop mounds of the ricotta into 4 serving bowls, surround with figs, and drizzle with chestnut honey. Serve with sherry.

PEANUT, BUTTER, AND JELLY LINZERTORTE

ONE 9-INCH CAKE

1½ cups flour

1½ cups unsalted roasted peanuts

¾ cup sugar

1 teaspoon baking powder

1 teaspoon ground cinnamon

½ teaspoon salt

12 tablespoons (1½ sticks) unsalted butter, cold

1 large egg plus 1 large yolk

1¼ cups Concord grape jelly

This is a dessert that I've wanted to make for a long time: a linzertorte that happily merges two of my favorite flavors, peanut and Concord grape. Baking pal Nick Malgieri raised an eyebrow when I told him about my idea, but I hope he will blush with pride when he tastes it, because I adapted this school yard–inspired version from his classic linzertorte recipe.

1   Position the rack in the center of the oven and preheat the oven to 350 degrees.

2   Measure the flour, peanuts, sugar, baking powder, cinnamon, and salt into the bowl of a food processor. Pulse until the peanuts are ground, but still slightly chunky.

3   Cut the cold butter into ½-inch pieces, add them to the dry ingredients, and pulse until the butter is broken up into tiny pieces. The mixture should resemble coarse cornmeal. Add the egg and the yolk, and process until the dough comes together in a ball. Press two-thirds of the dough with the heel of your hand into an even layer that covers the bottom of the pan and comes 1½ inches up the sides.

4   Spoon the Concord grape jelly evenly over the dough in the bottom of the pan.

5   On a lightly floured surface, roll the remaining third of the dough into ½-inch-round ropes. Lay the ropes in a criss-cross lattice pattern over the filling.

6   Butter the bottom of a 9-inch springform pan.

7   Bake the torte for 40 minutes, until it is a deep golden brown. Cool completely, then remove the sides of the pan and wrap the torte in plastic to mellow.

Note: The linzertorte can be stored at room temperature for up to 1 week, or wrapped securely in plastic and frozen for up to 2 months.

A DUO OF WINE GRAPE SORBETS

6 TO 8 SERVINGS

MUSCAT SORBET:
(makes 3 cups)

2 pounds muscat grapes
(about 3 cups juice)

¼ cup water

1 tablespoon sugar

2 tablespoons light corn
syrup

CONCORD SORBET:
(makes 3 cups)

2½ pounds Concord
grapes

¼ cup water

¼ cup sugar

2 tablespoons light corn
syrup

One of my favorite refreshments is a pair of icy grape sorbets—perfect after a rich dinner or on a blazing-hot Indian summer afternoon. When I was shopping for grapes at the market, I ran into Alan Tangren, former forager and current pastry chef at Chez Panisse. He asked what I was making. "Wine grape sorbets," I said. He peered into my basket and made a face when he saw Concord grapes. Apparently he wasn't convinced that Concord grapes were for winemaking. I told him about the numberless glasses of Manischewitz wine I had seen my relatives consume, but I don't think he was persuaded.

If you don't have an ice cream maker, freeze the grape juice in a shallow pan, then scrape with a soup spoon to make a granita.

1   To make the sorbets: Stem the grapes and put them in a large nonreactive saucepan with the water. Cover and cook until the grapes are juicy and soft, stirring occasionally. Pass the grapes through a food mill or press them through a mesh sieve set over a bowl to separate the seeds and skins from the pulp.

2   Whisk the sugar and corn syrup indicated for each variety of grape into the warm grape juice until dissolved. Chill thoroughly, then freeze in your ice cream maker according to the manufacturer's instructions.

MELON WITH THREE FLAVORED SYRUPS

4 SERVINGS

3 pounds melon (cantaloupe, honeydew, Crane, or other favorite melon; or a combination), peeled, seeded, and cut into pieces

THE CHARTREUSE-MINT SYRUP:

¼ cup sugar

1 cup water

1 cup packed fresh mint leaves, plus more for garnish

2 tablespoons green Chartreuse, or to taste

THE SAKE-AND-GINGER SYRUP:

1½-inch piece of fresh ginger (about 1½ ounces, unpeeled)

¾ cup sugar

6 tablespoons water

1 cup plus 2 tablespoons dry sake

Optional: Powdered red chili pepper for garnish

THE CHAMPAGNE-LIME SYRUP:

¾ cup sugar

½ cup water

Grated zest of 2 limes (see Note)

1 cup Champagne

Juice of ½ lime, or to taste

Look! *You* choose which of these three refreshing syrups you like best with your melon. Will it be the spicy sake-and-ginger syrup, the sophisticated Champagne-lime, or the herbal Chartreuse-mint?

1   **To make the Chartreuse-mint syrup:** In a small nonreactive saucepan, heat the sugar and water until the sugar is dissolved. Crush the mint leaves with your hand and add them to the syrup. Remove from the heat and cool completely. Remove the mint, squeezing to extract all the flavor, then stir in the Chartreuse.

2   Pour the syrup over one-third of the melon and refrigerate until thoroughly chilled, for at least 1 hour. (The melon with Chartreuse syrup can be chilled up to 8 hours ahead.)

3   **To make the sake-and-ginger syrup:** Thinly slice the ginger (no need to peel). In a small nonreactive saucepan, heat the sugar, water, sake, and ginger slices. Remove from the heat and cool completely. Remove the ginger slices.

4   Pour the syrup over another third of the melon pieces and refrigerate until thoroughly chilled, for at least 1 hour. (The melon with sake-and-ginger syrup can be chilled up to 12 hours ahead.)

5   **To make the Champagne-lime syrup:** In a small nonreactive saucepan, heat the sugar, water, and lime zest until the sugar is dissolved. Remove from the heat, cover, and cool to room temperature. Strain out the zest, and stir the Champagne and lime juice into the syrup.

6   Pour the syrup over the remaining third of the melon and refrigerate until thoroughly chilled, for at least 1 hour. (The melon with Champagne-lime syrup can be chilled up to 8 hours ahead.)

Serving: Spoon each kind of melon into beautiful glasses. Garnish the melon with Chartreuse-mint syrup with mint strewn on top. Garnish the melon with ginger syrup with a light sprinkling of chili pepper, if desired.

Note: If you wish, you can chop the lime zest very fine and leave it in the Champagne-lime syrup.

WATERMELON AND SAKE SORBET

4 cups seeded water-
melon chunks (1-inch
pieces)

²⁄₃ cup sugar

10 tablespoons dry sake

Optional: Fresh lime juice

It's okay to use an inexpensive sake for this recipe. The very fancy, more costly brands usually have labels you won't be able to decipher anyway—unless you can read Japanese.

1   In a food processor or blender, whiz the watermelon chunks with the sugar and sake until smooth.

2   Taste, and if you wish, add a few drops of lime juice to adjust the sweetness to your liking.

3   Chill thoroughly, then freeze in an ice cream maker according to the manufacturer's instructions.

POMEGRANATE GRANITA

8 SERVINGS

4 cups fresh unsweetened
pomegranate juice (see
Note)

¼ cup sugar

Seeds of 1 pomegranate,
for garnish

Years ago at a Baker's Dozen meeting, I made friends with Rochelle Huppin-Fleck, then a pastry chef at a restaurant called Granita. While scoping out the weight lifters at nearby Venice Beach, Rochelle had the brilliant idea of adapting the weight lifters' baggy pants for professional chefs to wear. Thus was born her successful company, Chefwear, and now Rochelle no longer makes desserts—professionally, that is.

Raising a family at home while running a fast-growing business, Rochelle still finds time to juice pomegranates. And on a recent visit, she found time to jot down her most popular recipe for me, the pomegranate granita she used to make at Granita.

1   Mix the fresh pomegranate juice and sugar together in a mixing bowl until the sugar is dissolved. Taste, and add a bit more sugar if desired (but the juice should still be tangy).

2   Pour the mixture into a nonreactive 9 by 13-inch pan and place in the freezer. Check the mixture in 90 minutes. When the sides are partially frozen and there is a layer of ice formed on the top, use a fork and long strokes to scrape the partially frozen mixture from the top to the bottom of the pan. You will begin to create ice crystals. Return the pan to the freezer.

3   After 1 hour, check and repeat the scraping technique with a fork. Return the ice to the freezer. In another hour, repeat the scraping with a fork.

4   After the third scraping, all of the mixture should be frozen into crystals. Once all the pomegranate juice is scraped into crystalline "granita," you're done.

Serving: Serve in wine-glasses and sprinkle with fresh pomegranate seeds. This granita is also fantastic paired with vanilla ice cream.

Note: Fresh pomegranate juice is sometimes available at farmer's markets and at natural foods stores. Bottled unsweetened pomegranate juice from natural foods stores can be substituted.

I always go a little loony when the first cherries of the season start to hit the markets, and then I'm filled with anxiety until the first Bing cherries appear, black-red and crisp-tender and unbeatably the best. A little later in the summer, this wacko baker starts baking crisps in a frenzy, tossing freshly ripened peaches with the sprinkling of sugar necessary to enhance their essential peachiness— now that's my idea of fuzzy logic!

STONE FRUITS

CHERRY SORBET FOR DUM-DUMS WITH ALMOND DING

THE CHERRY SORBET:
(makes about 3 cups)

4 cups pitted cherries
(about 1½ pounds)

½ cup sugar

1 cup water

1 tablespoon fresh lemon juice

A few drops of almond extract

Optional: 1 tablespoon kirsch

THE ALMOND DING:

1 cup whole blanched almonds

½ cup sugar

2 tablespoons butter, salted or unsalted

¼ teaspoon coarse salt plus more for sprinkling

The cherry sorbet recipe is truly a snap: No ice cream machine is required, although you will need a food processor.

As for the oddly named almond candy that goes with it, I was dining out at Cindy Pawcyln's Mustards Grill in the Napa Valley when I was first served this terrific confection: whole almonds encased in crispy, buttery caramel, with just a touch of salt. I loved it even more when I found out the name.

1   **To make the cherry sorbet:** Heat the cherries with the sugar, water, and lemon juice in a nonreactive saucepan. Simmer for about 3 minutes, until the cherries soften and begin to release their juices.

2   Remove from the heat and add a few drops of almond extract and the kirsch, if using. Pour the cherries and the syrup into a small bowl and freeze until solid, which will take at least 2 hours.

3   Once the cherry mixture has frozen solid, remove it from the bowl and put it into a food processor. Process until completely smooth. Serve immediately in tall glasses, or return the sorbet to the freezer until ready to serve. It will have a nice texture for at least a few hours. If it has become too firm, remove it from the freezer a few minutes before serving.

4   While the sorbet is setting up, use the time to make the almond ding. Lightly grease a baking sheet. Put the almonds, sugar, butter, and salt in a medium-size saucepan or skillet. Cook over medium heat, stirring gently (stirring too much encourages crystallization), until the liquid begins to darken slightly.

5   Keep cooking, and when the liquid is a rich amber color (like dark coffee with a touch of cream), pour the mixture out onto the greased baking sheet. Do not spread it out. Sprinkle evenly with a hefty pinch of coarse salt. Cool completely, then break into bite-sized pieces and serve with the cherry sorbet.

Note: Store ding for up to 1 week in an airtight container.

CHERRY ALMOND COBBLER

8 SERVINGS

THE FILLING:

5 cups sweet fresh cherries, stemmed and pitted (about 2 pounds)

2 tablespoons sugar

Juice of ½ lemon

THE TOPPING:

7 ounces almond paste

⅓ cup sugar

8 tablespoons (1 stick) unsalted butter, at room temperature

1 large egg, at room temperature

½ teaspoon vanilla or almond extract

1 cup flour

1½ teaspoons baking powder

½ teaspoon salt

½ cup whole milk

I once visited a large-scale automated cherry-processing plant in France that had a huge cherry-pitting room filled with Dumpster-size bins full of cherry pits. The multitude of pits were shipped to the nearby Lenôtre bakery to weight tart shells during baking. The French are indeed masterful with their thrift.

At home you may not be able to dedicate a whole room to this purpose, and you probably won't have pits by the ton to dispose of, but do consider dedicating an old red corduroy shirt to be your cherry-pitting camouflage gear. And if you want to, save up your pits, and use them for pie weights too.

1   Position the oven rack in the center of the oven and preheat the oven to 350 degrees.

2   **To make the filling:** Arrange the cherries in an even layer in a shallow 2-quart baking dish. Toss the cherries with 2 tablespoons of sugar and the lemon juice.

3   **To make the topping:** Beat together the almond paste and the ⅓ cup of sugar, either in the bowl of an electric mixer or by hand, until the almond paste is finely broken up. Beat in the butter, then beat in the egg and the vanilla or almond extract.

4   In a separate bowl, whisk together the flour, baking powder, and salt. Stir half of the dry ingredients into the butter and almond paste mixture, stir in the milk, and finally the remaining dry ingredients.

5   Spoon the batter evenly over the cherries in the baking dish and bake for 45 minutes, until the topping is golden brown and a toothpick inserted into the center comes out clean.

Serving: Serve warm or at room temperature, with whipped cream (page 35) or vanilla ice cream.

Variations: For a mango-blackberry almond cobbler, make a filling with 10 small mangoes (about 5 pounds), peeled, pitted, and sliced, 2 pint baskets of blackberries, 2 tablespoons brown sugar, $\frac{1}{2}$ teaspoon vanilla extract, and the juice of 1 lemon.
    For the filling of a mixed-berry almond cobbler, use 5 cups of mixed berries, about $\frac{1}{4}$ cup sugar, and the juice of $\frac{1}{2}$ lemon.

CHOCOLATE BREAD WITH SAUTÉED CHERRIES

ONE 9-INCH LOAF, 10 TO 12 SERVINGS

THE BREAD:

3 ounces bittersweet chocolate (see Note)

4 tablespoons (½ stick) unsalted butter

1 envelope dry yeast (not instant)

¾ cup tepid water

3 tablespoons sugar

2 cups bread flour (see Note)

¾ teaspoon salt

3 tablespoons unsweetened cocoa powder (see Note)

1 large egg

½ teaspoon vanilla extract

½ cup chocolate chips, or 3 ounces bittersweet chocolate, chopped into ½-inch pieces

½ cup walnuts, hazelnuts, or pecans, toasted and coarsely chopped

THE CHERRIES:
(makes 4 to 6 servings)

2½ cups fresh cherries, stemmed and pitted (about 1 pound)

2 tablespoons sugar

1 tablespoon cognac or kirsch

I love any bread with all sorts of chunky stuff in it. Seeds, dried fruits, nuts—you name it, I want it in my bread. And I've been intrigued by the challenge of creating a loaf of bread that has a tremendous amount of chocolate flavor and yet is simple to make. Of course it has to have chunks of toasted nuts and chocolate pieces.

If you've never made bread before and are timid to try, this recipe will put you at ease. Besides, it's really, really good: whether soaking up the juices from sautéed cherries, as here, or lightly toasted for breakfast with a thin smear of cream cheese . . . or for the true chocolate lover, topped with a little Nutella!

Consider making the sautéed cherries as an accompaniment not just to this recipe but to the brownies on page 134 or to Lindsey's Italian-style cheese on page 199.

1   To make the bread: Coarsely chop the bittersweet chocolate. Cut the butter into small pieces. Melt the chocolate and butter in a small bowl set over simmering water, gently stirring until smooth. Remove from the heat and set aside.

2   In the bowl of an electric mixer, stir together the yeast and the tepid water along with a big pinch of the sugar. Let stand for 5 minutes.

3   Using the dough hook attachment of the electric mixer, mix in the remaining sugar, the flour, salt, cocoa powder, egg, vanilla, melted chocolate, and butter.

4   Beat for 5 minutes, until the dough is smooth (it will be very soft, not stiff). Beat in the chocolate chips and the

chopped nuts. Cover the bowl with plastic wrap and let the dough rise in a warm place for 1½ hours.

5   Butter a 9-inch loaf pan. Briefly knead the dough and form it into an elongated oval, like a big brown potato. Put the dough in the prepared pan, stretching the dough gently into the corners. Let rise for 30 minutes.

6   Ten minutes before baking the bread, position the oven rack in the center of the oven and preheat the oven to 350 degrees.

7   Bake the loaf for 50 minutes. Remove from the oven and let stand in the pan for 20 minutes. Tilt the loaf out of the pan onto a cooling rack and cool completely.

8   **To sauté the cherries:** Heat the cherries in a skillet over medium heat with the 2 tablespoons of sugar, shaking frequently, until the cherries have softened and are heated through. After a few minutes the cherries will release their juices. (If necessary, add a few tablespoons of water.) Remove from the heat and stir in cognac or kirsch.

Note: The cherries can be prepared up to 5 days in advance, if refrigerated, and will actually improve as they stand. I like to make extra when cherries are abundant at the market and freeze them in small containers, rewarming them throughout the year and serving them spooned over ice cream or sorbet.

I find that this bread is better made with bread flour, which is available in natural foods stores and well-stocked supermarkets. If you can't find it, all-purpose flour works well, but the loaf will be somewhat denser than one made with bread flour.

CHOCOLATE AND FRESH CANDIED CHERRY CAKE WITH ROASTED ALMOND CRÈME ANGLAISE

ONE 9-INCH CAKE

THE CHERRIES:

½ pound fresh (or frozen) pitted cherries (about 1½ cups)

1 cup water

1 cup sugar

THE CAKE BATTER:

12 ounces bittersweet or semisweet chocolate

12 tablespoons (1½ sticks) unsalted butter

6 large eggs, separated

2 tablespoons kirsch

3 tablespoons sugar

THE CRÈME ANGLAISE:
(makes 3 cups)

½ cup sliced almonds

2 cups whole milk

⅓ cup sugar

Pinch of salt

6 large egg yolks

¼ teaspoon almond extract

A few years ago I was preparing to teach a series of holiday baking classes around the country, and since my Web site had been inundated with requests for fruitcake recipes, I decided to do a candied cherry and chocolate fruitcake. I presumed that good-quality Italian candied cherries (the kind labeled Agrimonte or Amarena) would be easy to find at any well-stocked supermarket.

As the classes neared their dates, the schools started calling me to report that they couldn't find any candied cherries. Fortunately, I was able to determine that frozen cherries were available just about everywhere. Quick-candied using the method below, they worked very well, and everyone's holiday baking was safe. (The next year, of course, most of the markets were well stocked with Italian candied cherries once again.)

1 **To candy the cherries:** Put the cherries in a saucepan with a capacity of at least 4 quarts (the juices may foam up). Add the water and sugar and cook over medium-high heat for 15 to 20 minutes, until the juices are thickened and syrupy. Do not overcook or the cherries will caramelize and taste "cooked." (To check their progress during cooking you may need to remove the pan from the heat and let the foam subside.)

2 When the cherries are candied, drain over a bowl, reserving the syrup, and cool. Once the cherries have cooled, chop them coarsely.

3 Position the oven rack in the center of the oven and preheat the oven to 325 degrees. Butter a 9-inch springform pan.

4 **To make the cake batter:** Cut the chocolate and butter into roughly ½-inch pieces. In a large bowl set over simmering

water, melt the chocolate and butter together. Stir in ½ cup of the reserved cherry syrup.

5   Remove from the heat and add the egg yolks, kirsch, and chopped cherries.

6   Whip the egg whites until they are foamy. When they begin to hold their shape, whip in the 3 tablespoons of sugar, and keep beating until they form soft peaks that hold their shape when you lift the whip. Do not overbeat.

7   Fold the whites into the chocolate mixture just until there are no streaks of egg white visible. Transfer the batter to the prepared springform pan and bake for 45 minutes.

8   **To make the crème anglaise:** Toast the almonds in a 325-degree oven for about 7 minutes, stirring once, until nicely browned.

9   Warm together the milk, toasted almonds, sugar, and salt in a medium-size heavy-duty saucepan. Remove from the heat, cover, and let steep for 1 hour.

10   Prepare an ice bath for cooling the crème anglaise: Nest a medium-size bowl in a larger bowl partly filled with ice and water.

11   Whisk the egg yolks together in a bowl. Gradually whisk in the almonds and milk and pour the mixture into a saucepan.

Note: This cake can be made up to 3 days in advance and kept at room temperature. The crème anglaise can be made and stored, covered, in the refrigerator, for up to 3 days.

12   Cook over medium heat, stirring constantly with a heat-proof utensil until the custard begins to thicken and coat the spoon. Do not boil. Pour the custard through a strainer into the bowl in the ice bath. Add the almond extract and stir until cool. Refrigerate until ready to serve.

PEACHES IN RED WINE

4 SERVINGS

¾ cup sugar

2 cups fruity red wine,
such as Merlot, Zinfandel,
or Beaujolais

4 ripe peaches, yellow and
white, if possible

Resist serving these with anything else. They deserve
to be savored by themselves.

1   In a bowl, whisk the sugar into the red wine until completely dissolved. (Superfine or "baker's sugar" works very well
here.)

2   Peel the peaches, cut them in half, and remove the pits.
Cut the peaches into 1-inch-thick slices and submerge them in
the wine. Taste and add more sugar if desired. Chill for at least
4 hours.

Serving: Divide the peach slices and wine among 4 shallow bowls.
You can prepare the peaches in wine up to 8 hours in advance and
keep them chilled until ready to serve.

Variation: Use yellow and white nectarines instead of peaches.
No need to peel the nectarines.

PEACH AND AMARETTI CRISP

8 SERVINGS

THE FILLING:

8 peaches (about 3 pounds), peeled and cut into ¼-inch slices (8 cups)

2 tablespoons granulated sugar

1 tablespoon flour

1 teaspoon vanilla extract or ½ teaspoon almond extract

THE TOPPING:

¾ cup flour

½ cup firmly packed light brown sugar

¼ cup granulated sugar

¾ cup crushed amaretti cookies (about 16 cookies)

1 teaspoon ground cinnamon

½ cup almonds, toasted

8 tablespoons (1 stick) unsalted butter, cut into ½-inch pieces and chilled

I once heard that the heir to an amaretti factory fortune was kidnapped for ransom. In my imagination I pictured him leaving a trail of amaretti crumbs in the forest to lead the authorities to his rescue. I can't guarantee that this strategy will work if you're kidnapped, but if you leave a trail of crumbs that leads to this crisp, you can be certain a crisp search-and-rescue party will follow.

1   Position an oven rack in the center of the oven and lay a sheet of aluminum foil on the rack below to catch drippings. Preheat the oven to 375 degrees.

2   **To make the filling:** Mix the peach slices with the granulated sugar, flour, and vanilla or almond extract. Transfer the peaches to a shallow 2-quart baking dish.

3   **To make the topping:** In a food processor, pulse together the flour, the brown and granulated sugars, amaretti, and cinnamon until the amaretti are in very small bits. Add the almonds and pulse until the nuts are in small pieces.

4   Add the pieces of butter and pulse until the butter is finely broken up. Continue to pulse until the topping no longer looks sandy and is just beginning to hold together.

5   Distribute the amaretti topping evenly over the peaches and bake the crisp for 40 to 50 minutes, until the edges are bubbling and a knife inserted into the center pierces the fruit easily.

Serving: Serve warm with a cold pitcher of heavy cream or with vanilla ice cream.

Note: The amaretti topping can be made ahead and refrigerated in a sealed plastic bag for up to 1 week, or frozen for up to 6 months. I like to keep a batch on hand, frozen and ready for a last-minute dessert.

Variation: For a berry crisp, toss 6 to 8 cups mixed berries (quartered strawberries, raspberries, blackberries, and blueberries) with $\frac{1}{3}$ cup sugar, 2 tablespoons flour, and a squirt of lemon juice. Cover with just enough topping to hide the fruit and freeze the rest.

PEACH SEMIFREDDO

8 SERVINGS

Here's a super-duper way to use lots of peaches. This is a great dessert to bring to a summertime picnic or barbecue: easy to assemble in advance—and even easier to eat.

THE KIRSCH SYRUP:

1 cup water

⅓ cup sugar

6 tablespoons kirsch

THE PEACH FILLING:

2 pounds ripe peaches (6 to 8)

3 to 4 tablespoons sugar

THE MASCARPONE FILLING:

2 cups homemade mascarpone (page 216 or see Variation on page 175 for making filling with store-bought mascarpone)

¼ cup sugar

1 teaspoon vanilla extract

1 sponge cake, 11 by 17 inches (page 128), cooled

3 ripe peaches

1 tablespoon sugar

12 amaretti cookies, crushed

1   **To make the kirsch syrup:** Heat the water and sugar together in a small saucepan until the sugar is dissolved. Stir in the kirsch and set aside.

2   **To make the peach filling:** Peel, halve, and remove the pits from the peaches. Cut them into ¼-inch-thick slices and toss them in a bowl with the sugar (how much depends on their sweetness) until juicy. Use your hands or a potato masher to break up the slices and encourage juiciness. The finished mixture should be very wet with large visible pieces of peaches.

3   **To make the mascarpone filling:** Whip the mascarpone or heavy cream until it begins to hold its shape. Stir in the sugar and vanilla.

4   Cut 2 layers in the sponge cake to fit a deep 2-quart glass baking dish.

5   To assemble the semifreddo, spread ½ cup of the mascarpone over the bottom of the baking dish. Set a layer of cake over the mascarpone. Soak the cake with half of the kirsch syrup. (It may seem like a lot, but it will all soak in.)

6   Spread the peach filling over the soaked cake. Spread 1¼ cups mascarpone over the peaches. Add the remaining cake layer and soak it with the remaining syrup. Spread the remaining mascarpone over the cake. Refrigerate, uncovered, for 30 minutes. Cover the cake with plastic wrap and keep chilled until ready to serve.

Serving: Peel, halve, and pit the 3 peaches and toss them with the 1 tablespoon of sugar. Either scatter the peach slices over the top of the cake, then sprinkle with crushed amaretti, or serve each plated portion with a scattering of peach slices and crushed amaretti.

Note: The semifreddo can be made up to 1 day before serving.

Variation: To make mascarpone filling using store-bought mascarpone: Stir $\frac{1}{4}$ cup milk, heavy cream, or half-and-half into 1 cup mascarpone. Whip $\frac{3}{4}$ cup heavy cream until it holds very soft peaks, then stir in $\frac{1}{4}$ cup sugar and 1 teaspoon vanilla extract. Fold the whipped cream into the lightened mascarpone.

PEACHES POACHED IN WINE SYRUP

4 SERVINGS

One 375 ml. bottle sweet
dessert wine, such as
Moscato, Gewürztraminer,
or Riesling

½ cup honey

1 cup water

Two ½-inch-wide strips
of lemon zest

½ vanilla bean

4 ripe peaches

I love to peel warm peaches. When the skins slip off
they reveal an unblemished rosy-hued blush that
reminds me of a baby's bottom.

1   In a medium-size saucepan with a 4-quart capacity, heat
together the wine, honey, water, and lemon zest. Split the
vanilla bean lengthwise, add it to the liquid, and bring the mixture to a boil.

2   Add the peaches and reduce the heat to a simmer. Cook
for about 20 minutes, until the peaches are tender all the way
to the pit when poked with a sharp paring knife.

3   Remove the peaches from the syrup with a slotted
spoon, and continue to cook the syrup until it is reduced by
about one half.

4   Slip the skins off the peaches and set each peach on a
plate, stem end down. Ladle syrup over the peaches and serve.

Serving: Serve warm or at room temperature with crisp cookies
or caramelized brioche (page 194).

APRICOT AND MARZIPAN TART

ONE 9-INCH TART, 8 SERVINGS

THE DOUGH:

1 cup flour

½ cup sliced almonds

¼ cup granulated sugar

⅛ teaspoon salt

8 tablespoons (1 stick) unsalted butter, chilled

1 large egg yolk

THE ALMOND TOPPING:

½ cup flour

⅓ cup firmly packed light brown sugar

⅓ cup (3 ounces) almond paste, crumbled

¼ cup sliced almonds

4 tablespoons unsalted butter (½ stick), chilled

THE FRUIT FILLING:

12 to 14 medium apricots (about 1 pound)

1 tablespoon cornstarch

¼ cup granulated sugar

I adapted this superbly yummy tart from a recipe by my baking pal Dede Wilson. I met Dede at a breakfast buffet at a culinary conference. Confronted by a huge table gloriously overloaded with all sorts of smoked salmon, kippers, trout, and other smoked fishes, I searched in vain for plain cream cheese and a bagel. I heard a distant voice, like an echo of my thoughts, asking in a tone of desperation, "Where are the bagels and cream cheese?" I knew right then we would be fast friends. (I will not eat smoked fish on a muffin!)

Dede demonstrated her version of this tart on the *Today* show, and she brought me back a small slice that had obviously made the trip from a New York City studio to her New England kitchen. It may have had a rough journey home in her handbag, but it was one of the best things I ever ate.

1   **To make the dough:** In the bowl of a food processor, pulse together the flour, almonds, granulated sugar, and salt until the nuts are finely ground. Cut the butter into ½-inch pieces and add them to the almond mixture. Pulse the processor until the mixture resembles coarse meal. Add the egg yolk and process until the dough comes together.

2   Use the heel of your hand to press the dough over the bottom and up the sides of a 9-inch tart pan with a removable bottom. Pierce 16 times with a fork and chill for at least 1 hour.

3   To prebake the tart shell, position the oven rack in the center of the oven and preheat the oven to 400 degrees. Bake the crust for 18 minutes, until deep golden brown. Midway

through baking, press down on the dough with the back of a metal spatula. When done, remove the pan from the oven to cool. Turn the oven down to 375 degrees.

4   **To make the topping**: With your fingers, mix together the flour, brown sugar, almond paste, and almonds. Cut the butter into $\frac{1}{2}$-inch pieces and work it into the mixture until the butter pieces are about the size of corn kernels. Set aside.

5   **To make the fruit filling**: Halve the apricots and remove the pits. Cut the apricots into $\frac{1}{2}$-inch slices, and toss them in a bowl with the cornstarch and granulated sugar.

6   Assemble the tart by spreading the apricot slices over the crust and evenly sprinkling the almond topping over them. Bake for 30 minutes.

Serving: Serve warm or at room temperature.

Variations: For raspberry-apricot marzipan tart, add 1 cup of raspberries or blackberries to the apricot filling. For plum marzipan tart, substitute $1\frac{1}{4}$ pounds of plums for the apricots and thicken with 1 tablespoon plus 1 teaspoon cornstarch. (Since plums are very juicy, don't slice them until you are ready to assemble and bake the tart.)

NECTARINE AND BLUEBERRY COBBLER
WITH BIG FLUFFY BISCUITS

You'll notice that this dessert is very low in the f-word (fat, that is), since I use buttermilk and only a modest amount of butter in the biscuits. So you don't have to feel any guilt about enjoying this with a rewarding scoop of melting vanilla ice cream. You'll also notice that these biscuits are much fluffier than traditional biscuits. The fluffiness I especially like because the biscuits soak up more of the tasty juices from the fruit.

THE FRUIT FILLING:

7 medium or 9 small nectarines (about 3 pounds)

6 tablespoons sugar

2 teaspoons fresh lemon juice

2 teaspoons flour

1 teaspoon vanilla extract

One 6-ounce basket of blueberries

THE BISCUITS:

1½ cups flour

1 teaspoon baking powder

¼ teaspoon baking soda

¼ teaspoon salt

2 teaspoons sugar plus more for sprinkling

4 tablespoons (½ stick) unsalted butter, frozen

⅔ cup buttermilk

1 large egg yolk

1 teaspoon milk

1   Position the oven rack in the center of the oven and preheat the oven to 375 degrees.

2   **To make the fruit filling:** Cut the nectarines in half, remove the pits, and cut the fruit into ½-inch slices. In a large, deep mixing bowl, toss the nectarines together with the sugar, lemon juice, flour, vanilla, and blueberries.

3   Transfer the fruit mixture to a 2-quart baking dish and bake in the oven for 40 minutes, stirring once during baking. (I recommend putting a layer of aluminum foil on the rack under the baking dish to catch any juices that may bubble over.) Remove the baking dish from the oven.

4   **To make the biscuits:** Mix together the flour, baking powder, baking soda, salt, and 2 teaspoons sugar. Using the largest holes on a box grater, grate the frozen butter into the flour mixture. Stir in the buttermilk until the dry ingredients are just moistened. Spoon the biscuit batter over the nectarines in 6 roughly equal mounds.

5   Mix the egg yolk with the milk and dab the top of each mound liberally with the egg wash. Sprinkle with a nice dusting of sugar and pop the cobbler back into the oven for 20 to 25 minutes, until the biscuits are browned.

Serving: Serve the cobbler warm with vanilla ice cream or a pitcher of very cold heavy cream.

Variations: Substitute peaches for the nectarines (but be sure to peel them). Substitute a 6-ounce basket of raspberries or blackberries for the blueberries or $1\frac{1}{2}$ cups of pitted cherries.

NECTARINE AND RASPBERRY UPSIDE-DOWN GINGERBREAD

Everyone knows that the whole point of an upside-down cake is to present a homey and delicious caramelized amalgam of fruit and topping embedded in a warm, buttery cake. My favorite part is licking the warm gooey bits that remain in the pan—with my fingers, of course.

THE TOPPING:

4 tablespoons (½ stick) unsalted butter

¾ cup firmly packed light brown sugar

4 medium nectarines (about 1½ pounds)

1 cup raspberries

THE GINGERBREAD CAKE:

1½ cups flour

2 teaspoons ground ginger

1 teaspoon baking soda

1 teaspoon ground cinnamon

½ teaspoon ground cloves

½ teaspoon salt

8 tablespoons (1 stick) unsalted butter, at room temperature

½ cup granulated sugar

½ cup mild molasses

2 large eggs, at room temperature

¼ cup milk

Whipped cream (page 35) or vanilla ice cream, for serving

1   To make the topping: Melt the 4 tablespoons of butter in a 10½-inch cast-iron skillet or a 9 by 2-inch round cake pan. Stir in the brown sugar until moistened and remove from the heat. (The topping will be a bit lumpy, which is fine.) Cool.

2   Distribute the raspberries over the melted brown sugar in the pan. Halve the nectarines, remove the pits, and cut the fruit into ½-inch slices. Arrange the slices on top of the raspberries in overlapping concentric circles.

3   Position the oven rack in the center of the oven and preheat the oven to 350 degrees.

4   To make the gingerbread cake: Whisk together the flour, baking soda, ginger, cinnamon, cloves, and salt. In the bowl of an electric mixer, or by hand, beat the 1 stick butter and granulated sugar together until light and fluffy. Beat in the molasses. (The batter may look curdled, which is fine.)

5   Scrape down the sides of the mixer, then add the eggs, one at a time.

6   Stir in half of the dry ingredients, then the milk, then the remaining dry ingredients. Spread the batter over the fruit in the pan and bake the cake for about 50 minutes (if using a cast-iron skillet) or 55 minutes (if using a cake pan).

Serving: Allow cake to cool for about 15 minutes, then remove from the pan by running a knife around the edge of the pan to loosen the cake. Invert a cake plate over the cake pan and flip both the cake and the plate simultaneously. Remove the cake pan, slice, and serve warm. If you are going to serve the cake later, don't lift off the cake pan until you are ready to serve. This will keep the cake warm for about 1 hour. Add whipped cream or vanilla ice cream.

Variations: For cranberry upside-down gingerbread, substitute 3½ cups (one 12-ounce bag) of cranberries for the nectarines and raspberries.

For a pear upside-down gingerbread, use 3 peeled and cored firm pears, cut into ½-inch slices.

For an orange version, add ½ teaspoon ground cardamom to the melted butter and brown sugar. Peel 4 navel or blood oranges, then slice them crosswise into ½-inch slices.

For a plum or pluot upside-down rendition, instead of the nectarines, use 8 medium-size plums or pluots (about 1 pound), pits removed and cut into ½-inch slices.

SPICED PLUM STREUSEL CAKE WITH TOFFEE GLAZE

THE TOPPING:

5 medium-size ripe plums (about ¾ pound)

1 cup sliced almonds

2 tablespoons flour

⅓ cup firmly packed light brown sugar

½ teaspoon ground cinnamon

½ teaspoon ground cardamom

1½ tablespoons butter, melted

THE CAKE:

8 tablespoons (1 stick) unsalted butter, at room temperature

¾ cup granulated sugar

1½ cups flour

½ teaspoon baking powder

½ teaspoon baking soda

1½ teaspoons ground cardamom

½ teaspoon ground cinnamon

½ teaspoon salt

2 large eggs, at room temperature

1 teaspoon vanilla extract

½ cup buttermilk

"Streusel" is a word that comes to us from German and means something strewn or scattered. Strewing is not confined to Germans, however, as long as you do it in the comfort and privacy of your own kitchen.

1 **To make the topping:** Halve the plums, remove the pits, and cut each one into 8 slices. Set aside. Crumble together the sliced almonds, flour, brown sugar, spices, and melted butter with a fork or your fingers, making sure the almonds are dispersed in small pieces.

2 Position the oven rack in the center of the oven and preheat the oven to 350 degrees. Butter a 9-inch springform pan.

3 **To make the cake:** With an electric mixer, or by hand, beat the butter and granulated sugar until light and fluffy, 3 to 5 minutes.

4 With a whisk, mix together the flour, baking powder, baking soda, cardamom, cinnamon, and salt.

5 Add the eggs, one at a time, to the butter and sugar, stopping occasionally to scrape down the sides of the bowl. Stir in half of the dry ingredients, the vanilla, and buttermilk, and finally the remaining dry ingredients. Mix until just combined.

6 Transfer the batter into the prepared springform pan. Smooth the top and press the plum slices into the batter. Sprinkle the streusel topping over the cake.

2 tablespoons butter

3 tablespoons dark brown sugar

3 tablespoons heavy cream

Big pinch of salt

¼ teaspoon vanilla extract

7   Bake the cake for 55 minutes, until the top is nicely browned and a toothpick inserted in the center comes out clean. Cool completely on a wire rack before glazing. When cool, remove the sides of the pan.

8   **To make the glaze:** Cut the butter into small pieces and melt it in a small saucepan with the dark brown sugar, heavy cream, and salt. Bring to a boil, reduce the heat, and boil gently for 1 minute. Remove from the heat and cool completely. Once cool, stir in the vanilla. Spoon the glaze over the cooled cake, encouraging some to drip down the sides.

PLUM, NECTARINE, AND BLACKBERRY CHARLOTTE

8 SERVINGS

I like to use a glass pan when I make a charlotte so I can watch the bottom (which will become the top) get nice and browned.

THE BREAD LAYER:

3 tablespoons unsalted butter, melted

1 tablespoon granulated sugar

12 slices firm-textured white bread (about a ¾-pound loaf)

THE FRUIT FILLING:

3 medium-size plums

3 medium-size nectarines

1 tablespoon unsalted butter

Two 6-ounce baskets of blackberries

¼ cup firmly packed light brown sugar

1 tablespoon fresh lemon juice or kirsch

½ teaspoon almond extract

Apricot or peach jam, strained, for glazing the charlotte

Vanilla ice cream, for serving

1   **To make the bread layer:** Brush a glass or nonreactive 8-inch square baking pan with some of the melted butter. Sprinkle the granulated sugar into the pan, tilting the pan to coat the sides.

2   Cut the bread slices into pieces to fit the bottom and sides of the pan in a single layer of bread. (It will make slicing and serving the baked charlotte easier if you use large pieces of bread rather than small scraps.) Brush the cut pieces with melted butter on one side and line the pan with the bread, buttered side down. Do not allow any bread to extend over the top. Reserve some bread and butter for a final layer of bread pieces to cover the fruit filling.

3   **To make the fruit filling:** Halve the plums and nectarines and remove the pits. Cut the fruits into large dice.

4   In a 12- to 14-inch skillet, melt the 1 tablespoon butter over medium-high heat. Add the diced fruit and the blackberries and cook until they begin to release their juices. Stir in the brown sugar and cook for 15 to 20 minutes, stirring frequently, until the fruit is cooked through and the juice from the fruit is very thick and syrupy, about the consistency of honey. Remove from the heat and stir in the lemon juice or kirsch and the almond extract.

5   Position the oven rack in the lower third of the oven and preheat the oven to 375 degrees.

6   Spoon the fruit filling into the bread-lined pan. Cover the fruit with a layer of pieces of bread and brush the bread with melted butter. Bake the charlotte for 30 to 40 minutes, until the bread is dark golden brown. Remove from the oven and cool in the pan about 30 minutes.

Serving: Invert a serving platter over the pan and flip the pan and the platter. Lift off the pan and brush the charlotte with the strained jam. Cut into rectangles and serve with vanilla ice cream.

THREE-SEED SHORTCAKES WITH
PLUMS AND RED BERRIES

8 SERVINGS

I love anything with seeds in it: I'm a regular seed demon. If I go to a bakery and I see seeds, that's what I get. In this recipe, three seeds may sound like at least two seeds too many, but believe me, they harmonize beautifully in concert with the plums and berries. You'll see.

THE PLUM-AND-BERRY COMPOTE:

6 medium-size ripe plums (about I pound)

½ cup sugar

I cup water

I vanilla bean, split lengthwise

I cup strawberries

½ cup raspberries

THE SHORTCAKES:

2 cups flour

3 tablespoons poppy seeds

2 tablespoons sesame seeds, toasted

2 tablespoons flax seeds (see Note)

Grated zest of I lemon

¼ cup sugar

2 teaspoons baking powder

½ teaspoon baking soda

½ teaspoon salt

8 tablespoons (I stick) unsalted butter, cut into ½-inch pieces and chilled

¾ cup buttermilk

I egg yolk

I teaspoon milk

2 cups whipped cream (page 35)

I **To make the compote:** Halve the plums and remove the pits. Slice each plum into 8 wedges (or 6, if the plums are small). Bring the sugar, water, and vanilla bean to a boil in a medium-size saucepan.

2 Add the plum slices to the sugar syrup and simmer for 3 minutes. Remove from the heat, cover, and let stand until the syrup has cooled to room temperature.

3 Hull the strawberries, cut them into quarters, and mix them in with the plums. In a food processor, purée half of the mixture and stir the purée into the fruit. Stir in the raspberries.

4 Position the oven rack in the center of the oven and preheat the oven to 400 degrees. Lightly butter a baking sheet or cover it with parchment paper.

5 **To make the shortcakes:** Mix together the flour, the poppy, sesame, and flax seeds, the lemon zest, and the sugar, baking powder, baking soda, and salt. Cut the butter pieces into the dry ingredients, either by hand or with an electric mixer or a food processor. Once the pieces are the size of corn kernels, stir in the buttermilk until the dough comes together.

6 On a lightly floured surface, pat or roll the dough into a flat piece ¾ inch thick. Using a 2½- to 3-inch round biscuit cutter, cut the dough into 8 biscuits. (You may need to gather the scraps and reroll them to make 8.)

7   Place the biscuits on the prepared baking sheet. Make the egg wash by mixing the egg yolk with the milk. Brush the tops liberally with the egg wash.

8   Bake the biscuits for 20 minutes, until nicely browned on top. Remove from the oven and cool.

Serving: Split the biscuits in half. Spoon whipped cream between the biscuit layers and serve with a mound of the juicy compote.

Note: Flax seeds are available in natural foods stores, usually in bulk.

YEASTED PLUM TART WITH
RED WINE-PLUM SAUCE

THE TART:

3 tablespoons whole milk

2 teaspoons dry yeast
(not instant)

¼ cup plus ¼ cup sugar

2 large eggs, at room
temperature

1½ teaspoons vanilla
extract

1½ cups flour

¾ teaspoon salt

6 tablespoons (¾ stick)
unsalted butter, cut into
½-inch pieces, at room
temperature

5 medium-size plums
(about 1 pound), pitted
and cut into ½-inch slices

**THE RED WINE-PLUM
SAUCE:**

½ cup dry red wine

1 plum, pitted and diced
into ¼-inch pieces

¼ cup sugar

Variation: Add 1 cup of
raspberries or blackber-
ries to the sauce either
before or after it's
puréed. Taste, and add
more sugar if necessary.

Many fledgling bakers tell me they are scaredy-cats making desserts that rise, but that's the yeast of their prob-
lems. In fact, this tart is a snap to make. It's plummy,
moist, and cheery, and people are crazy about it.

1   Liberally butter a 9½-inch springform pan.

2   **To make the tart:** In the bowl of a standing electric mixer,
stir together the milk and the yeast. Add in ¼ cup of sugar, the
eggs, and vanilla. Add the flour and salt and beat well with the
paddle attachment for 1 minute. Add the butter and beat for
another minute. Scrape the dough into the prepared pan, cover
with plastic wrap, and let rise in a warm place for 2 hours.

3   After 2 hours, dampen your hands and press down on the
dough, spreading it to the edges of the pan. Leaving a ½-inch
border, arrange the plum slices over the top of the dough in
concentric circles, pressing the plums firmly into the dough.
Sprinkle the fruit and edges with the remaining ¼ cup of
sugar (it seems like a lot, but trust me). Let the tart stand for
30 minutes.

4   Position the oven rack in the center of the oven and preheat the oven to 350 degrees.

5   Bake the tart for 40 minutes, until it is lightly browned
and the center feels slightly firm when you press it.

6   **To make the red wine-plum sauce:** Warm the red wine,
plum pieces, and ¼ cup sugar in a small nonreactive saucepan
and bring to a simmer. Simmer until the plums are tender.
Transfer the mixture to a blender and purée.

Serving: Cut the tart (still warm, preferably) into wedges and
serve them with a generous amount of sauce.

Juicy! Juicy, juicy, juicy. What more can you say about the most perfect things that nature has ever created? Smush them, sweeten them, toss them with other fruits—or savor them one by one right out of the basket. Just don't eat them all before you get to the kitchen!

BERRIES

CARAMELIZED BRIOCHE WITH SUGARED STRAWBERRIES IN RED WINE

8 TO 10 SERVINGS

THE BRIOCHE:

1 envelope dry yeast
(not instant)

2 tablespoons milk,
at room temperature

3 tablespoons sugar
plus ¼ cup granulated
or crystal sugar

2 large eggs, at room
temperature

1½ cups flour

¾ teaspoon salt

6 tablespoons (¾ stick)
unsalted butter, cut into
small pieces, at room
temperature, plus 1 tablespoon unsalted butter,
melted for brushing over
the brioche before baking

**THE SUGARED
STRAWBERRIES:**

3 cups fruity red wine,
such as Merlot, Zinfandel,
or Beaujolais

1½ cups granulated sugar

4 pint baskets strawber-
ries, hulled and quartered
(about 2 quarts)

This recipe was inspired by a galette that Jacques Pépin made with me, which quickly became one of my favorites. Don't be afraid of making brioche. It takes literally two minutes to assemble and is easier than just about anything I know. Be sure to have all ingredients at room temperature—unless your room is in an igloo.

1   **To make the brioche:** Sprinkle the yeast over the milk in the bowl of an electric mixer fitted with the paddle attachment or in a medium-size bowl. Stir in the 3 tablespoons sugar, eggs, flour, and salt. Beat vigorously for 1 minute. Add the 6 tablespoons soft butter and continue to beat for another minute, until there are no visible pieces of butter in the dough.

2   Scrape the dough into a ball within the bowl and cover with plastic wrap. Set in a warm place to rise for 1½ hours.

3   Line a baking sheet with parchment paper or lightly butter the baking sheet. Scrape the dough onto the center of the prepared baking sheet. Dampen your hands and gently press the dough into a 12-inch circle. (It doesn't need to be perfectly round, but make sure it's about ⅓ inch thick.) Brush the top with 1 tablespoon melted butter and sprinkle with ¼ cup granulated or crystal sugar. Let it rise again for 20 minutes.

4   To bake the brioche, position the oven rack in the center of the oven and preheat the oven to 425 degrees.

5   Bake the brioche for 10 to 12 minutes, until the sugar on top is crunchy and the center springs back when you press it lightly.

6   Remove from the oven and slide the brioche onto a baking rack until ready to serve.

7   **To prepare the sugared strawberries in red wine syrup:** Whisk together the wine and sugar until the sugar is dissolved. Add the quartered strawberries and let marinate for 30 to 60 minutes before serving.

8   In a small bowl, stir a few tablespoons of the sweetened wine into the cornstarch to dissolve it and make a slurry.

9   Drain the rest of the red wine liquid off the strawberries into a skillet and gently boil over medium heat until the liquid is reduced by about half. Add the cornstarch slurry and simmer for 1 to 2 minutes, until the syrup is thickened slightly. Remove the syrup from the heat and cool completely. Once cool, add the strawberries.

Serving: Cut the brioche into wedges while still warm and serve with a generous spoonful of strawberries. The brioche can be made up to 8 hours in advance and rewarmed for 5 minutes or so before serving in a preheated 350-degree oven.

STRAWBERRIES IN RED WINE SYRUP WITH ALMOND MERINGUE BASKETS

8 SERVINGS

Although these baskets are easiest to make using a pastry bag, you could simply drop 8 fluffy mounds of meringue on the baking sheet and make an indentation in each one with the back of a soup spoon dipped in water.

THE MERINGUE BASKETS:

4 large egg whites

¼ teaspoon almond extract

Pinch of salt

½ cup granulated sugar

⅓ cup powdered sugar

About ½ cup sliced almonds

THE STRAWBERRIES IN RED WINE SYRUP:

3 cups fruity red wine, such as Merlot, Zinfandel, or Beaujolais

1½ cups granulated sugar

4 pint baskets strawberries, hulled and quartered (about 1 quart)

1 tablespoon cornstarch

2 cups whipped cream (page 35) or 1 pint vanilla ice cream or fruit sorbet

1   Preheat the oven to 200 degrees and line two baking sheets with parchment paper.

2   **To make the meringue baskets:** In the bowl of an electric mixer, begin to whip the egg whites with the almond extract and the salt at medium speed. Once they become foamy, increase the speed to medium-high and continue to whip until they begin to hold their shape.

3   While the mixer is whipping, gradually add the ½ cup granulated sugar and continue to whip until the meringue is shiny and very stiff. Remove the bowl from the mixer.

4   Put the powdered sugar in a sifter or strainer and sift it over the meringue, folding it in with a rubber spatula as you sift. Transfer the meringue to a pastry bag fitted with a ½-inch plain tip.

5   Pipe eight 4-inch meringue disks on the prepared baking sheets by holding the pastry bag and squeezing to make a solid spiral of meringue for the bottoms. Once you've piped all 8 disks, build up the sides of the baskets by squeezing out meringue with a circular motion, creating a nice pocket.

6   Gently press the sliced almonds onto the meringue baskets.

7   Bake for 2 hours, turn off the oven, and let the meringues remain in the oven for 1 more hour. Remove from the oven and cool.

8   **To prepare the strawberries in red wine syrup:** Whisk the red wine and sugar together in a nonreactive large bowl until the sugar is dissolved. Add the quartered strawberries and let marinate for 30 to 60 minutes.

9   In a small bowl, stir a few tablespoons of the sweetened wine into the cornstarch to dissolve it and make a slurry.

10   Drain the rest of the red wine liquid off the strawberries into a nonreactive skillet and gently boil over medium heat until the liquid is reduced by about half. Add the cornstarch slurry and simmer for 1 to 2 minutes, until the syrup is thickened slightly. Remove the syrup from the heat and cool completely. Once cool, add the strawberries.

Serving: Fill each meringue basket with whipped cream, ice cream, or sorbet. Spoon a generous amount of strawberries and red wine syrup over and around each meringue.

Note: The meringues can be made up to 1 week in advance, cooled, and stored in an airtight container. The strawberries in red wine syrup can be made up to 8 hours beforehand and refrigerated or not, as you like.

LINDSEY'S HONEYED STRAWBERRIES

AL FORMAGGIO

THE *FORMAGGIO*
(Italian-style cheese):

1 cup heavy cream

2 tablespoons sugar

½ tablespoon fresh lemon juice

2 tablespoons Marsala

THE STRAWBERRIES:

1 pint basket strawberries

1 tablespoon honey, or to taste

Lindsey Shere was not just the head pastry chef at Chez Panisse, she was also its voice of reason. She once remarked to a co-worker, "You know, if you added more sugar to that, it would be sweeter." I mean, who could argue with that logic?

Here is one of her perfectly simple recipes. If you want it sweeter, you know what to do.

1   **To make the Italian-style cheese:** Use a whisk or an electric mixer to whip the heavy cream and the sugar until the cream holds soft peaks. Beat in the lemon juice and Marsala, and continue to whip until the cream is thick enough to hold its shape.

2   Line a strainer with a few layers of cheesecloth and set the strainer over a bowl deep enough so that there is at least 1 inch of space between the bottom of the strainer and the bowl.

3   Scrape the cream into the cheesecloth, drape with plastic wrap, and refrigerate for between 24 and 48 hours.

4   **To prepare the strawberries:** Rinse, hull, and quarter the berries and toss them with the honey.

Serving: Spoon some of the Italian-style cheese into stemmed goblets and top with the honeyed strawberries. Serve with Lemon Quaresimali (page 110) or Peppery Chocolate-Cherry Biscotti (page 138).

STRAWBERRY BAVARIAN WITH ORANGE-RHUBARB SAUCE

THE BAVARIAN:

2 pint baskets
strawberries

¾ cup sugar

2 tablespoons vodka
or kirsch

4 teaspoons unflavored
gelatin

1 cup cold water

1¼ cups heavy cream

½ teaspoon vanilla extract

THE ORANGE-
RHUBARB SAUCE:

1 cup orange juice

½ cup sugar

¾ pound rhubarb stalks,
trimmed of leaves and
root ends and diced into
¼-inch pieces

The strawberry-rhubarb combination is a classic, usu-ally in pies or crisps. Here the tangy rhubarb sauce pairs perfectly with the lush creaminess of a straw-berry Bavarian, which is sliced like a cake. The sauce is also splendid with a very different kind of dessert, the polenta cake on page 46.

1   To make the Bavarian: Hull the berries and thinly slice them into a large bowl. Add the sugar and the vodka or kirsch, and mash the berries with your hands (or pulse in a food processor) until the berries are juicy but still slightly chunky. Set aside.

2   In a saucepan, sprinkle the gelatin over the cold water and let stand 5 minutes. Stir the gelatin over very low heat until it is dissolved. Whisk the gelatin into the mashed straw-berries.

3   Lightly oil a 2-quart round baking dish (such as a souf-flé dish) or a 9-inch nonstick (nonreactive) springform pan.

4   Whip the heavy cream with the vanilla until it forms soft, drooping peaks (it should not be too stiff). Fold the whipped cream into the strawberry mixture. Taste, and add more sugar if necessary. Transfer the Bavarian mixture into the prepared dish or pan and refrigerate for at least 6 hours.

5   To make the orange-rhubarb sauce: Bring the orange juice, sugar, and diced rhubarb to a boil in a nonreactive saucepan, reduce the heat, and simmer until the rhubarb is tender, about 10 minutes. Remove from the heat and mash the rhubarb with the back of a fork, leaving some chunks.

6   To unmold the Bavarian, run a sharp knife around the edge to release it from the sides of the mold. Remove the sides of the springform pan or baking dish. Invert a serving plate over the Bavarian. Hold both the serving plate and the bavarian, and flip them simultaneously. Fold a dish towel on the counter and tap the Bavarian on the countertop to encourage it to slide out of the dish. (If it doesn't, soak a dish towel in hot water, wring it dry, and wrap it around the outside of the dish for a minute. Unmold again.)

Serving: Slice the cold Bavarian into wedges and serve with a generous spoonful of the orange-rhubarb sauce.

Note: The Bavarian can be wrapped in plastic and stored in the refrigerator for up to 2 days.

BERRIES ROMANOFF WITH ICED SOUR CREAM

4 SERVINGS

THE BERRIES ROMANOFF:

¾ cup Triple Sec or Curaçao (not blue Curaçao)

½ cup sugar

Grated zest of 1 orange

5 to 6 cups (about 3 half-pint baskets) mixed berries (strawberries, hulled and quartered, blackberries, blueberries, and raspberries)

THE ICED SOUR CREAM:

⅔ cup whole milk

⅓ cup sour cream

¼ cup sugar

2 teaspoons vodka

It doesn't look as if the Romanoff family will ever get the throne of Russia back, but their lofty name is permanently attached to this supremely simple dessert—so simple that you can toss it together at the last minute when you don't want to go off on some lunatic dessert bender. The berries traditionally need no accompaniment, but if you have an ice cream maker and a little time, they are delicious with this simple iced sour cream.

1   **To prepare the berries:** In a medium-size mixing bowl, whisk together the Triple Sec or Curaçao, sugar, and orange zest until the sugar is dissolved. (Superfine or baker's sugar dissolves most easily.)

2   Stir in the berries and marinate at room temperature for at least 1 hour, stirring gently once or twice.

3   **To make the iced sour cream:** Mix together the whole milk, sour cream, sugar, and vodka in a blender. Freeze in your ice cream maker according to the manufacturer's instructions.

Serving: Spoon the berries into 4 stemmed wineglasses, add a scoop of the iced sour cream, then pour the Triple Sec and berry juice over each dessert.

BOYSENBERRY TURNOVERS

THE DOUGH:

1 cup flour

1 tablespoon sugar

½ teaspoon salt

5 tablespoons unsalted butter, cut into ½-inch cubes and chilled

2 ounces cream cheese

3 tablespoons ice water

THE FILLING:

2¼ cups (about one and a half 6-ounce baskets) boysenberries

2 tablespoons sugar

Grated zest of 1 lemon

1 tablespoon flour

1 egg yolk

1 teaspoon milk or heavy cream

Granulated or coarse sugar, for sprinkling over the turnovers

Of all the techniques of dessert-making, rolling out dough is the one people are most skittish about. I hate to admit it, but when faced with buttery flaky pastry dough, even I still pick up my rolling pin with a bit of trepidation. Not this dough, though. The cream cheese makes it easy to roll, and this dough won't crack or crumble.

My partiality for boysenberries dates back to my childhood obsession with the tabletop syrup carousels at Aunt Jemima's Pancake House on the Berlin Turnpike in Connecticut, which featured boysenberry syrup along with an astonishing array of other flapjack-friendly flavors. There's certainly no substitute for the winy, inky, unctuous flavor of fresh plump boysenberries, but there's no reason you can't make turnovers with blackberries, raspberries, or a mixture.

1   **To make the dough:** Mix together the flour, sugar, and salt. With an electric mixer or food processor, mix in the butter pieces until they're about half their original size. Add the cream cheese and continue to mix until the pieces of butter are the size of corn kernels.

2   Mix in the ice water, stirring just until the dough comes together. Wrap in plastic wrap and shape into a thick, flat square. Refrigerate for at least 1 hour.

3   To bake the turnovers, position the oven rack in the center of the oven and preheat the oven to 400 degrees. Line a baking sheet or a nonstick baking mat with parchment paper.

4   **To make the filling:** In a medium-size bowl, toss the boysenberries, sugar, lemon zest, and flour.

5   Divide the dough into 4 square pieces. On a lightly floured surface, roll each one into a 5-inch square. Place ¼ of the berry mixture in the center of each square of dough. Brush the inside edges of the dough with water and fold the dough over the berries, encasing them in a triangular turnover. Pinch or crimp the edges securely. (Leave no openings or too much juice may run out and burn on the baking sheet.)

6   Beat together the egg yolk and the milk or cream, brush each turnover with the egg glaze, and sprinkle each one liberally with granulated or coarse sugar. Poke a slit in the top of each turnover with a sharp knife.

7   Place the turnovers on the prepared baking sheet and bake for 20 minutes. Serve warm or at room temperature.

BLACKBERRY FINANCIERS

12 SMALL CAKES

7 tablespoons unsalted butter

1¾ cups sliced almonds, preferably blanched

½ cup granulated sugar

½ cup powdered sugar

5 tablespoons flour

⅛ teaspoon salt

4 large egg whites

½ teaspoon almond extract

One 6-ounce basket blackberries

Note: Store cooled cakes in an airtight container for up to a week.

Variations: Substitute peach, nectarine, or plum slices for the blackberries (you may want to peel the peaches first). Cut the fruit into ½-inch slices and lay them over the top of each little cake before baking. You can also sprinkle the top of each cake with untoasted sliced almonds before baking.

I like to think of these little cakes as food for financiers—the cartoon kind with big bulging sacks with dollar signs on them, like the Monopoly man. You'll want to make a substantial deposit of blackberries into each one (although there are no penalties for investing in raspberries or blueberries). And if you eat these warm from the oven, there's no penalty for early withdrawal.

1   Position the oven rack in the center of the oven and preheat the oven to 400 degrees. Butter a 12-cup muffin tin.

2   In a skillet, heat the butter until it begins to sizzle. Continue to cook over low heat until the edges begin to darken and the butter gives off a nutty aroma. Remove from the heat. (The butter may sputter and splatter while cooking. If you want, place an overturned colander over the pan to protect yourself.)

3   In a food processor, grind the almonds with the granulated and powdered sugars, the flour, and the salt. While the processor is running, gradually pour in the egg whites and add the almond extract. Stop the machine, and add the warm butter, pulsing as you pour until the batter is just mixed.

4   Divide the batter evenly among the buttered muffin cups and poke 3 or 4 blackberries into each cake. Bake for 18 minutes, until puffy and deep golden brown. (Although I recommend that you follow the baking time indicated, I once baked a batch of these financiers and by accident left them in the turned-off oven for almost 2 days, after which they were still moist and buttery in the center!) Let stand a few minutes, then remove them from the pan and cool on a rack.

BLACKBERRY AND LEMON GRATIN

4 SERVINGS

2 cups half-and-half

6 tablespoons sugar

Pinch of salt

Grated zest of 2 lemons

Two 6-ounce baskets of blackberries

1 tablespoon cornstarch

6 large egg yolks

¼ cup firmly packed dark brown sugar

I don't mean to be a spoiler, but I never really cared for the typical *clafoutis*, a French creation of fruit baked in a thin batter and served from the baking dish. Maybe it helps to fantasize that you're sitting in the French countryside, having a picnic in the springtime, but to me, most clafoutis are flabby pudding-like fruit-and-custard creations. So this is my answer: a tangy, lemony gratin with sweet blackberries baked under a brown sugar glaze.

If you have individual shallow gratin dishes, by all means, this is the time to use them.

1   In a nonreactive saucepan, warm the half-and-half, sugar, salt, and lemon zest. Remove from the heat, cover, and let steep for 1 hour.

2   Distribute the blackberries in a 9- to 10-inch glass pie plate or a shallow baking dish. In a small bowl, whisk the cornstarch and egg yolks together until smooth.

3   Add a small amount of the warm lemon-infused cream mixture to the egg yolks, stirring constantly with a whisk. Pour the warmed egg yolks into the saucepan and cook over medium heat, stirring constantly, until the mixture thickens and just about comes to a boil. (You may need to whisk it a bit if it becomes lumpy, which is normal.) Strain the mixture over the blackberries in the pie plate.

4   Position the oven rack in the uppermost position of the oven and turn on the broiler. Evenly sprinkle the brown sugar over the custard and slide the gratin under the broiler for about 4 minutes, until the sugar is melted and the custard is bubbling at the edges.

Note: The custard can be made up to 2 days in advance and refrigerated. If using cold custard, the time under the broiler for the sugar to melt will be about 6 minutes.

Variations: Substitute 10 to 15 rose geranium leaves for the lemon zest. Steep for 1 hour, then strain out the leaves before cooking the custard.

Instead of blackberries, use 3 cups of blueberries or 3 cups mixed berries, such as raspberries, blueberries, blackberries, and boysenberries.

RANCH PANNA COTTA WITH BLUEBERRIES

THE PANNA COTTA:

1⅓ cups half-and-half
(or whole milk)

½ cup sugar

Grated zest of 2 lemons

2 cinnamon sticks

1 envelope unflavored
gelatin

3 tablespoons cold water

⅔ cup buttermilk

THE BLUEBERRIES:

4 cups fresh or frozen
blueberries

½ cup sugar

¼ cup gin

When I was working on this recipe, I was talking on the phone to my friend, chef James Ormsby. I told him I was making ranch panna cotta. There was a long pause at the other end, and then he said, "Ranch, like ranch salad dressing?" No, I'm not one of those pastry chefs who does all those weird combinations. My ranch panna cotta is based on a drink with the rather unfortunate name of "fermented milk" that is served at Rancho la Puerta spa in Mexico. The drink—buttermilk accented with cinnamon and lemon—was actually delicious. (Surprisingly, although I didn't miss my nightly glass of wine at the spa, I would have given my first-born male child for a ladleful of chocolate sauce.)

1   **To make the panna cotta:** Warm the half-and-half (or milk), sugar, lemon zest, and cinnamon sticks in a nonreactive saucepan. Once the mixture begins to steam, remove it from the heat, cover, and let steep for 30 to 60 minutes.

2   In a medium-size bowl, sprinkle the gelatin over the cold water and let it soften for 5 minutes. Rewarm the infused half-and-half, then pour it through a strainer over the softened gelatin, stirring to dissolve it completely. Stir in the buttermilk. (The half-and-half mixture should not be steaming-hot at this point, or the buttermilk can separate. If it does, whisk it vigorously and it will become smooth.)

3   Lightly grease eight 4-ounce ramekins or 6-ounce custard cups with unflavored oil. Divide the panna cotta mixture evenly among the prepared ramekins and refrigerate for at least 4 hours.

4   **To prepare the blueberries:** Warm the berries in a saucepan with the sugar and gin, until they soften and release their juices. Remove from the heat and let stand until they cool to room temperature.

Serving: Run a sharp knife around the inside edge of each ramekin to release the panna cotta. Invert each one on a serving plate. Spoon the blueberries around and over the panna cotta.

MIXED BERRY PIE

ONE 10-INCH PIE, ABOUT 8 SERVINGS

A bubbling berry pie just out of the oven and cooling by an open window, ripe for swiping, is one of the silliest clichés of home baking. No city-dweller in his right mind would leave anything so valuable as a mixed berry pie on his windowsill.

THE DOUGH:

2¼ cups flour

2 tablespoons sugar

½ teaspoon salt

10 tablespoons (1¼ sticks) unsalted butter, cut into ½-inch cubes and chilled

4 ounces cream cheese, cut into ½-inch cubes and frozen

6 tablespoons ice water

THE FILLING:

1 pint basket strawberries, hulled and diced (2½ cups)

1 pint basket blackberries (2 cups)

One 6-ounce basket blueberries (1½ cups)

½ cup sugar

2 tablespoons cornstarch

1 tablespoon fresh lemon juice or kirsch

THE GLAZE:

1 egg yolk

1 teaspoon milk

1 tablespoon granulated or coarse sugar crystals, for sprinkling over the top crust

1   **To make the dough:** Mix the flour, sugar, and salt in a food processor or with a standing electric mixer. Add the butter. If using a food processor, pulse 5 times. In a mixer, mix until the pieces of butter are about half their original size.

2   Add the cream cheese cubes and pulse or mix until the pieces of butter and cream cheese are about the size of large peas. Add the ice water and mix until the dough comes together. Gather the dough together with your hands and separate into 2 pieces. One piece should be about ⅓ of the dough, the other twice as large. Flatten them into thick disks, wrap in plastic, and refrigerate for at least 30 minutes.

3   Position the oven rack in the center of the oven and preheat the oven to 400 degrees. (I recommend placing a sheet of foil on the rack under the pie to catch any dripping juices.)

4   On a lightly floured surface, roll the smaller disk of dough into a 13-inch circle. Fold the dough in half, then lay it over half of a 10-inch pie plate. Unfold the dough and coax it into the pie plate.

5   **To make the filling:** Mix the berries together with the sugar, flour, and lemon juice or kirsch. Spread the berry filling evenly in the pie plate. Roll the remaining disk of dough on a

lightly floured surface into a 15-inch circle. Brush the exposed edges of the pie dough in the pie plate with water. Drape the 15-inch circle of dough over the pie. Trim the dough circle so it overhangs by about 1½ inches. Tuck the overhanging dough under the lower pie dough and crimp the edges.

6 Make an egg glaze by beating together the egg yolk and milk. Brush the pie with the glaze and sprinkle the 1 tablespoon of sugar over the top. With the tip of a sharp knife, poke 4 slits in the dough around the top of the pie and one in the center.

7 Bake the pie for 50 to 55 minutes, until there is juice bubbling up through the center slit. Cool completely before cutting and serving.

MASCARPONE CHEESECAKE
WITH MIXED BERRIES

To me, cheesecake should not be light and delicate. It should be thick and rich, so thick that when I slide a mouthful from the fork, I leave a telltale toothy impression of the large gap between my front teeth.

Can't find mascarpone? Make it yourself! I love the thrill of making my own cheese at home on my stovetop. I think you will too.

THE CRUST:

1 cup graham cracker (or gingersnap) crumbs (about 7 whole graham crackers)

1 tablespoon sugar

2 tablespoons unsalted butter, melted

THE CHEESECAKE:

1 pound cream cheese, at room temperature

1¼ cups sugar

1 teaspoon vanilla extract

Grated zest of 1 lemon

5 large eggs, at room temperature

2 cups mascarpone (page 216)

THE MIXED BERRIES:

3 to 4 cups mixed berries (sliced strawberries, raspberries, blackberries, and blueberries)

3 tablespoons sugar, or to taste

1   Lightly grease the bottom and sides of a 9-inch spring-form pan. Wrap the underside and outside of the pan with a large sheet of aluminum foil (unless you're certain your pan is leakproof). Position the oven rack in the lower part of the oven and preheat the oven to 375 degrees.

2   **To make the crust:** Toss the graham cracker crumbs with the sugar and melted butter. Using a flat-bottomed glass, press the crumb mixture evenly into the bottom of the prepared springform pan. Bake the crust for 10 minutes. Remove from the oven and set the pan aside to cool. Reduce the heat to 325 degrees.

3   **To make the cheesecake:** Either by hand or with an electric mixer at medium speed, mix the cream cheese and sugar until there are no lumps. Add the vanilla and lemon zest.

4   Mix in the eggs, one at a time, until completely incorporated. If using an electric mixer, stop and scrape down the sides of the bowl as necessary. Stir in the mascarpone.

5   Pour the batter over the crust in the springform pan, then set the pan in a larger pan, such as a roasting pan. Pour enough warm water into the larger pan to reach about halfway up the sides of the springform.

6   Bake the cheesecake in the water bath for 55 minutes. Turn off the oven and leave the cake in the water bath in the oven for an additional 20 to 30 minutes, until it is still jiggly but in a solid mass. Remove from the water bath and cool completely on a wire rack. (Do not be tempted to cool a warm cheesecake in the refrigerator: The condensation will cause the cake to be soggy.) Refrigerate in the pan for at least 3 hours and up to 5 days.

7   Before serving, prepare the mixed berries by tossing them with the sugar until they become juicy.

Serving: Use a sharp thin knife to loosen the edges of the cheesecake from the pan. Remove the sides of the springform, then cut slices with a sharp knife dipped in warm water. Serve each slice with a big spoonful of the berries.

MASCARPONE

MAKES 2 CUPS

2 cups heavy cream

⅓ teaspoon tartaric acid
(*not* cream of tartar,
see Note)

Besides being great in cheesecake, a dollop of mascarpone is terrific served with a bowl of plump summer berries and sweetened peach slices.

1   Warm the cream in a saucepan until it reaches 180 degrees on an instant-read thermometer.

2   Remove from the heat and stir in the tartaric acid. Stir continuously for 2 minutes to dissolve the crystals.

3   Pour the mixture into a clean container, cover, and refrigerate for 12 hours.

Note: Tartaric acid is available at pharmacies and winemaking stores and can be ordered by mail from:

The Great American Spice Company
P.O. Box 80068
Fort Wayne, IN 46898
(888) 502-8058
www.americanspice.com

CASSIS TRUFFLES

ABOUT 30 TRUFFLES

8 ounces bittersweet or semisweet chocolate plus 5 ounces, for coating

½ cup heavy cream

3 tablespoons unsalted butter, at room temperature

3 tablespoons *crème de cassis* liqueur

¾ cup unsweetened cocoa powder

I like chocolate truffles to look like real truffles, as if freshly dug, so I never roll the scoops of chocolate filling into absolutely smooth spheres, although you can if you chill the scoops first. Either way, biting into one is an almost overwhelming flavor experience, one of the few chocolate and berry combinations that really works.

The best way to dip these is to line up the three elements: the plate holding the balls of truffle filling on the left, the bowl of melted chocolate in the center, and the pan of cocoa powder on the right. (If you're left-handed, you may reverse this.) Coat the truffles with your right hand and keep the other one free of chocolate. And, of course, make sure your hands are clean and dry before dipping.

1   Chop the 8 ounces of chocolate into small pieces, about ½ inch each. In a medium-size saucepan, bring the cream to a boil, remove from the heat, and gently stir in the chopped chocolate. Whisk in the butter until completely melted and stir in the liqueur. Pour the mixture into a shallow container, cover, and refrigerate until firm, at least 3 hours.

2   Scoop out truffles with a 1-inch melon baller. The best way to do this is to dip the melon baller in very hot water before each scoop, tap off the water, scoop a truffle, and release it onto a plate lined with plastic wrap. After you're done, use your hands to roll each truffle into a ball, then chill the truffles until firm, which should take only a few minutes.

3   Sift the cocoa into a pie pan or a similar-sized pan. Melt the remaining 5 ounces chocolate in a clean dry bowl.

4   Gather up some of the melted chocolate with your right hand. Use your left hand to pick up a truffle and drop it into your chocolate-covered right hand. Smear the truffle with melted chocolate, using only your right hand, then drop the truffle into the cocoa powder. Coat all the truffles this way. When done, shake the tray of cocoa around to coat the truffles completely. Put the truffles in a mesh strainer, and shake off any excess cocoa.

Note: These are best stored in the refrigerator, well wrapped, for no more than a week to 10 days. Leftover chocolate and cocoa powder can be reused.

TOMATO JAM WITH ROSEMARY COOKIES

2 CUPS JAM, ABOUT 24 COOKIES

THE JAM:

5 large ripe tomatoes (about 2¼ pounds)

2¼ cups sugar

2 to 3 grinds of black pepper

Big pinch of salt

1 teaspoon fresh lemon juice

THE ROSEMARY COOKIE DOUGH:

½ pound (2 sticks) unsalted butter, at room temperature

10 tablespoons sugar

2 large egg yolks

1½ tablespoons finely chopped fresh rosemary leaves

2 cups flour

¼ cup stone-ground cornmeal or polenta

½ teaspoon salt

When I was in school at the École Lenôtre near Paris, I took a course in confectionery. During the course, we made gumdrops, marshmallows, lollipops, licorice whips, and all sorts of candies. At one point, our teacher abruptly departed from the candy curriculum and taught us how to make a batch of tomato jam, for reasons that were not entirely clear to me, since I speak barely a soupçon of French. I loved the jam, which was a yummy reminder that, botanically speaking, tomatoes are fruits. But I had no idea what to do with it.

Fortunately, television chef Joey Altman happened to be coming over to tape an episode on holiday candy-making in my kitchen. I gave him a taste of the jam, which he too loved, and he told me to sandwich it between rosemary shortbread. Normally I don't make trendy desserts with herbs, because the results are often yucky. But this shortbread, like the jam, is also delicious.

1   To make the tomato jam: Bring a large saucepan of water to a boil. Cut out the stem end of the tomatoes, then cut a shallow X on the opposite side. Plunge the tomatoes into the boiling water for 30 seconds. Remove the tomatoes from the water with a slotted spoon, cool briefly, and slip off their skins. Discard the water, but reserve the saucepan to cook the jam.

2   Cut the tomatoes in half at their equator and gently squeeze out the seeds and water. Dice the tomatoes into ½-inch pieces.

3   Put the diced tomatoes back into the large saucepan, stir in the sugar, and grind in the pepper. Cook the mixture over

low to medium heat, reducing the heat and stirring if the mixture foams up to the top of the pan.

4   When most of the liquid has cooked off, remove the pan from the heat and stir in the lemon juice. If using a candy thermometer, the temperature now will read 220 degrees. Let the jam cool thoroughly, to room temperature.

5   **To make the rosemary cookie dough:** Beat the butter and the sugar together, by hand or with an electric mixer, for 1 minute, just until smooth. Mix in the egg yolks, then the rosemary.

6   Stir in the flour, cornmeal or polenta, and salt. Mix until the dough is smooth and holds together. On a lightly floured surface, roll the dough into 2 cylinders, each about 6 inches long and 1¼ inches wide. Chill thoroughly.

7   To bake the cookies, adjust two oven racks to the upper and lower parts of the oven and preheat to 250 degrees. Line two baking sheets with parchment paper.

8   Slice the cookie dough into ¼-inch rounds (48 circles) and place them on the prepared baking sheets, spaced about ½ inch apart. Bake the cookies for about 12 minutes, rotating the baking sheets midway during baking, until the edges brown slightly. Remove the baking sheets from the oven and set them on wire racks to cool the cookies before filling.

9   Sandwich a scant ½ tablespoon of the tomato jam between 2 cookies.

Note: Leftover jam can be stored in the refrigerator for up to 6 months. The cookies will keep in an airtight container at room temperature for 2 to 3 days.

RECIPES BY TYPE

CANDIES AND NUTS

Almond Ding 162

Candied Orange 88

Candied Pecans 34

Cassis Truffles 217

Pistachio, Almond, and Cherry Bark 136

Salted Almonds 39

COOKIES

Coconut Flatties 58

Cranzac Cookies 147

Crispy Peanut Cookies 101

Lemon Quaresimali 110

Peppery Chocolate-Cherry Biscotti 138

Pineapple Coconut Cookies 65

Rosemary Cookies 220

CAKES AND BREADS

Absolute Best Brownies with Dried
  Cherries 134

Banana Cake with Mocha Icing and
  Coffee Crunchies 74

Blackberry Financiers 207

Buckwheat Cake 21

Caramelized Brioche 194

Chocolate and Fresh Candied Cherry
  Cake 168

Chocolate Bread 166

Chocolate Cherry Fruitcake 132

Chocolate Soufflé Cake 118

Date, Ginger, and Candied Pineapple
  Fruitcake 125

Hazelnut, Apricot, and Chocolate
  Dacquoise 145

Mascarpone Cheesecake 214

Nectarine and Raspberry Upside-Down
  Gingerbread 182

Papaya Cake 53

Peach Semifreddo 174

Plum, Nectarine, and Blackberry
  Charlotte 186

Polenta Cake 46

Prune, Coffee, Chocolate, and Amaretto
  Tiramisù 128

Prune Gâteau Basque 130

Ricotta Cake 88

Spiced Apple Charlotte 28

Spiced Plum Streusel Cake with
  Toffee Glaze 184

Syrian-Style Date-Nut Torte 124

Totally Orange Allspice Cake 86

PIES AND TARTS

Apple and Quince Tarte Tatin 30

Apple Tart with Whole-Wheat Express
  Puff Pastry 24

Apricot and Marzipan Tart 178

Apricot Filo Triangles 142

Boysenberry Turnovers 203

Brazil Nut, Date, and Ginger Tart 122

Free-Style Lemon Tartlets 105

Fresh Fig and Raspberry Tart with
  Honey 150

Lime Marshmallow Pie 98

Mango Tarte Tatin 63

Mixed Berry Pie 212

Peanut, Butter, and Jelly Linzertorte
  153

Pineapple Frangipane Tart 66

Rhubarb Tart with Almond Nougatine 48

ICE CREAMS, SORBETS, AND CUSTARDS

Anise-Orange Ice Cream 90

Apricot Ice Cream Tartufi 140

Bittersweet Chocolate Mousse 121

Blackberry and Lemon Gratin 208

Blood Orange Sorbet 84

Butterscotch Pudding 71

Caramelized Pineapple Flan 69

Cherry Sorbet for Dum-Dums 162

Chocolate-Tangerine Sorbet 97

A Duo of Wine Grape Sorbets 154

Frozen Caramel Mousse 39

Frozen Riesling Sabayon 83

Kiwi, Pineapple, and Toasted Coconut Baked Hawaii 55

Lemon-Ginger Crème Brûlée 108

Lime Cream Puffs with Sugared Almonds 102

Margarita Sorbet 101

Pear, Cherry, and Chocolate Bread Pudding 44

Pink Grapefruit Champagne Sorbet 104

Pomegranate Granita 159

Ranch Panna Cotta 210

Strawberry Bavarian 200

Superlemon Soufflé 112

Watermelon and Sake Sorbet 158

CRISPS, COBBLERS, AND SHORTCAKES

Apple and Pear Crisp with Polenta Topping and Grappa-Soaked Raisins 20

Cherry Almond Cobbler 164

Cornmeal Shortcakes 42

Gravenstein Apple and Blackberry Crisp 18

Nectarine and Blueberry Cobbler 180

Peach and Amaretti Crisp 172

Stilton Shortcakes 34

Three-Seed Shortcakes 189

COMPOTES AND POACHED FRUITS

Apples Poached in Cider 21

Berries Romanoff 202

Blackberries in Port 119

Coffee-Caramelized Bananas 71

Honey-Poached Pears 34

Marsala-Poached Pears Stuffed with Ricotta, Chocolate, Almonds, and Cherries 37

Melon with Three Flavored Syrups 155

Orange-Honey Fruit Salad 81

Peaches in Red Wine 171

Peaches Poached in Wine Syrup 176

Pear and Fig Chutney 121

Prunes, Cranberries, and Kumquats in Port 118

Saffron-Poached Pears 46

Sherry Glazed Pears 40

Spice-Baked Pears 42

Sugared Strawberries in Red Wine 194

Sautéed Cherries 166

SAUCES

Apricot Sauce 145

Chocolate Sauce 90

Cider Sabayon 28

Mango and Lilikoi Butter 76

Maple-Walnut Sauce 24

Orange-Rhubarb Sauce   200

Red Wine Syrup   197

Retsina Syrup   142

Roasted Almond Crème Anglaise   168

Rosy Rhubarb Sauce   88

Tangerine Butterscotch Sauce   94

White Chocolate Sauce   105

FRESH AND LEAN (NONFAT AND LOW-FAT DESSERTS)

Berries Romanoff   202

Blood Orange Sorbet   84

Blood Orange Soup   83

Cherry Sorbet for Dum-Dums   162

Cranzac Cookies   147

A Duo of Wine Grape Sorbets   154

Gingery Lemonade   115

Jellied Tangerine Juice   96

Kiwi, Pineapple, and Toasted Coconut Baked Hawaii   55

Marsala-Poached Pears Stuffed with Ricotta, Chocolate, Almonds, and Cherries   37

Melon with Three Flavored Syrups   155

Orange-Honey Fruit Salad   81

Peaches in Red Wine   171

Peaches Poached in Wine Syrup   176

Pink Grapefruit Champagne Sorbet   104

Pomegranate Granita   159

Quince Marmalade   33

Strawberries in Red Wine with Almond Meringue Baskets   197

Syrian-Style Date-Nut Torte   124

Tangerine Sorbet   97

Tomato Jam   220

Watermelon and Sake Sorbet   158

EASY

Berries Romanoff   202

Blackberry Financiers   207

Blood Orange Sorbet   84

Bostock   81

Caramelized Brioche   194

Cassis Truffles   217

Cherry Sorbet for Dum-Dums   162

Chocolate-Tangerine Sorbet   97

Cranzac Cookies   147

Gingery Lemonade   115

Homemade Ricotta with Fresh Figs and Chestnut Honey   152

Jellied Tangerine Juice   96

Lindsey's Honeyed Strawberries al Formaggio   199

Margarita Sorbet   101

Melon with Three Flavored Syrups   155

Peaches in Red Wine   171

Peaches Poached in Wine Syrup   176

Peppery Chocolate-Cherry Biscotti   138

Pink Grapefruit Champagne Sorbet   104

Rancho Panna Cotta   210

Strawberries in Red Wine Syrup with Almond Meringue Baskets   197

Syrian-Style Date-Nut Torte   124

Watermelon and Sake Sorbet   158

BIBLIOGRAPHY

Bertolli, Paul, with Alice Waters. *Chez Panisse Cooking.* New York: Random House, 1988.

Braker, Flo. *Sweet Miniatures: The Art of Making Bite-Size Desserts.* New York: William Morrow, 1991.

González, Elaine. *The Art of Chocolate.* San Francisco: Chronicle Books, 1998.

Herbst, Sharon Tyler. *The New Food Lover's Companion.* New York: Barron's, 1995.

Hirigoyen, Gerald, with Cameron Hirigoyen. *The Basque Kitchen: Tempting Food from the Pyrenées.* New York: HarperCollins, 1999.

Lenôtre, Gaston. *Lenôtre's Desserts and Pastries.* New York: Barron's, 1977.

Malgieri, Nick. *Chocolate: From Simple Cookies to Extravagant Showstoppers.* New York: HarperCollins, 1998.

——. *How to Bake.* New York: HarperCollins, 1995.

McGee, Harold. *On Food and Cooking: The Science and Lore of the Kitchen.* New York: Charles Scribner's Sons, 1984.

Miller, Carey D., Katherine Bazore, and Mary Bartow. *Fruits of Hawaii.* Honolulu: University of Hawaii Press, 1965.

Pépin, Jacques. *Jacques Pépin's The Art of Cooking.* New York: Alfred A. Knopf, 1988.

Wolfert, Paula. *The Cooking of South-West France.* New York: Harper & Row, 1983.

INDEX

Page numbers in *italics* indicate illustrations.

Allspice Orange Cake, with Brown Sugar Glaze,
    86-87
Almond(s):
    Apricot and Marzipan Tart, 178-79
    Blackberry Financiers, *206,* 207
    Bostock, Orange-Honey Fruit Salad with,
        80, 81-82
    Buckwheat Cake with Apples Poached in
        Cider, 21-22, *23*
    Cherry Cobbler, 164-65
    Ding, Cherry Sorbet for Dum-Dums with,
        162-63
    Lemon Quaresimali, 110-11
    Mango-Blackberry Cobbler, 165
    Marsala-Poached Pears Stuffed with
        Ricotta, Chocolate, Cherries and,
        36, 37-38
    Meringue Baskets, Strawberries in Red
        Wine Syrup with, *196,* 197-98
    Mixed-Berry Cobbler, 165
    Nougatine, Rhubarb Tart with, 48-49
    Peach and Amaretti Crisp, 172-73
    Pear, Cherry, and Chocolate Bread Pudding,
        45
    Pineapple Frangipane Tart, 66-67
    Pistachio, and Cherry Bark, 136-37
    Roasted, Crème Anglaise, Chocolate
        and Fresh Candied Cherry Cake with,
        168, 169-70
    Salted, Frozen Caramel Mousse with Sherry-
        Glazed Pears, Chocolate and, 39-40, *41*
    Spiced Plum Streusel Cake with Toffee
        Glaze, 184-85
    Sugared, Lime Cream Puffs with, and
        Coconut-Rum "Kaya," 102-3
Amaretti and Peach Crisp, 172-73
Amaretto, Prune, Coffee, and Chocolate
    Tiramisù, 128-29
Anise-Orange Ice Cream Profiteroles with
    Chocolate Sauce, 90-93, *91*
Apple(s):
    Charlotte, Caramelized, 29
    Charlotte, Spiced, with Cider Sabayon, 28-29
    and Cranberry Crisp, 19
    Gravenstein, and Blackberry Crisp, 18-19
    and Mince Crisp, 19
    and Pear Crisp with Polenta Topping and
        Grappa-Soaked Raisins, 20
    Poached in Cider, Buckwheat Cake with,
        21-22, *23*
    and Quince Tarte Tatin, 30-31
    selecting and storing, 10
    Tart with Whole-Wheat Express Puff Pastry
        and Maple-Walnut Sauce, 24-27
Apricot(s):
    Filo Triangles with Retsina Syrup, 142-43
    Hazelnut, and Chocolate Dacquoise with
        Apricot Sauce, *144,* 145-46
    Ice Cream *Tartufi,* 140-41
    and Marzipan Tart, 178-79
    Sauce, Hazelnut, Apricot, and Chocolate
        Dacquoise with, *144,* 145-46
    selecting and storing, 10, 12

Baked Hawaii, Kiwi, Pineapple, and Toasted
    Coconut, 55-57
Banana(s):
    Cake with Mocha Icing and Coffee
        Crunchies, 74-75
    Coffee-Caramelized, Butterscotch Pudding
        with, 71-73, *72*
    and Mango Napoleons with Lime Custard
        and Coconut Flatties, 58-61, *59*
    selecting and storing, 11
Bark, Pistachio, Almond, and Cherry, 136-37
Bavarian, Strawberry, with Orange-Rhubarb
    Sauce, 200-201
Beating, 7
Berry(ies), 194-221
    Crisp, 173
    Mixed-, Almond Cobbler, 165
    Mixed, Mascarpone Cheesecake with, 214-15
    Mixed, Pie, 212-13
    Red, Three-Seed Shortcakes with Plums
        and, *188,* 189-90
    Romanoff with Iced Sour Cream, 202
    washing, 5
    see also specific berries
Biscotti, Peppery Chocolate-Cherry, 138-39
Biscuits. *See* Cobblers; Shortcakes

Blackberry(ies):
Apricot Marzipan Tart, 179
Crushed, Mango Tarte Tatin with, *62,* 63-64
Financiers, *206,* 207
and Gravenstein Apple Crisp, 18-19
and Lemon Gratin, 208-9
Mango Almond Cobbler, 165
and Peach Cobbler, 181
Plum, and Nectarine Charlotte, 186-87
in Port, 119
Red Wine–Plum Sauce, Yeasted Plum Tart
with, 191
selecting and storing, 11
see also Berry(ies)
Blueberry(ies):
and Nectarine Cobbler with Big Fluffy
Biscuits, 180-81
Ranch Panna Cotta with, 210-11
selecting and storing, 11
see also Berry(ies)
Boiling, 7
Bostock, Orange-Honey Fruit Salad with,
80, 81-82
Boysenberry Turnovers, 203-4, *205*
Brazil Nut, Date, and Ginger Tart, 122-23
Bread:
Bostock, Orange-Honey Fruit Salad with,
80, 81-82
Chocolate, with Sautéed Cherries, 166-67
Pudding, Pear, Cherry, and Chocolate,
44-45
see also Charlottes
Brioche, Caramelized, with Sugared
Strawberries in Red Wine, 194-95
Brownies with Dried Cherries, 134-35
Brown Sugar Glaze, 86-87
Buckwheat:
Cake with Apples Poached in Cider,
21-22, *23*
Crêpes with Tangerine Butterscotch Sauce,
94-95
Butter:
greasing pans with, 5
Peanut, and Jelly Linzertorte, 153
at room temperature, 8

Butterscotch:
Pudding with Coffee-Caramelized Bananas,
71-73, *72*
Tangerine Sauce, Buckwheat Crêpes with,
94-95

Cakes:
Banana, with Mocha Icing and Coffee
Crunchies, 74-75
Buckwheat, with Apples Poached in Cider,
21-22, *23*
Chocolate and Fresh Candied Cherry,
with Roasted Almond Crème Anglaise,
168, 169-70
Chocolate Cherry Fruitcake, *127,* 132-33
Chocolate Soufflé, with Prunes, Cranberries,
and Kumquats in Port, 118-19
Date, Ginger, and Candied Pineapple
Fruitcake, 125-26, *127*
Date-Nut Torte, Syrian-Style, 124
Mascarpone Cheesecake with Mixed
Berries, 214-15
Nectarine and Raspberry Upside-Down
Gingerbread, 182-83
Orange Allspice, with Brown Sugar Glaze,
86-87
Papaya, with Coconut Glaze, 53-54
Peach Semifreddo, 174-75
Peanut, Butter, and Jelly Linzertorte, 153
Polenta, with Saffron-Poached Pears, 46-47
Prune, Coffee, Chocolate, and Amaretto
Tiramisù, 128-29
Ricotta, with Candied Orange and Rosy
Rhubarb Sauce, 88-89
Spiced Plum Streusel, with Toffee Glaze,
184-85
Sponge, 128
see also Charlottes
Cakes, little:
Blackberry Financiers, *206,* 207
Brownies with Dried Cherries, 134-35
Hazelnut, Apricot, and Chocolate Dacquoise
with Apricot Sauce, *144,* 145-46
Peach, Plum, or Nectarine Financiers, 207

Candied:
    Cherries, 169
    Lemons, Quick, 114
    Orange Peel, Quick, 88
    Pecans, 34
Candies and confections:
    Almond Ding, 162–63
    Almond Nougatine, 48–49
    Cassis Truffles, 217–18, *219*
    Coffee Crunchies, 75
    Pistachio, Almond, and Cherry Bark, 136–37
Candy thermometers, 4
Caramel:
    Mousse, Frozen, with Sherry-Glazed Pears, Chocolate, and Salted Almonds, 39–40, *41*
    Pineapple, 69
    Rum, 58, *59,* 60
Caramelized:
    Apple Charlotte, 29
    Brioche with Sugared Strawberries in Red Wine, 194–95
    Coffee-, Bananas, Butterscotch Pudding with, 71–73, *72*
    Pineapple Flan, *68,* 69–70
Cassis Truffles, 217–18, *219*
Champagne:
    Lime Syrup, 155–57, *156*
    Pink Grapefruit Sorbet, 104
Charlottes:
    Caramelized Apple, 29
    Plum, Nectarine, and Blackberry, 186–87
    Spiced Apple, with Cider Sabayon, 28–29
Chartreuse-Mint Syrup, 155–57, *156*
Cheese:
    Formaggio, Honeyed Strawberries *al,* 199
    Manchego, Quince Marmalade with, *32, 33*
    Stilton Shortcakes with Candied Pecans and Honey-Poached Pears, 34–35
    see also Mascarpone; Ricotta
Cheesecake, Mascarpone, with Mixed Berries, 214–15
Cherry(ies):
    Almond Cobbler, 164–65
    Chocolate Biscotti, Peppery, 138–39
    Chocolate Fruitcake, *127,* 132–33

Dried, Brownies with, 134–35
Fresh Candied, and Chocolate Cake with Roasted Almond Crème Anglaise, *168,* 169–70
Jam Gâteau Basque, 130–31
Marsala-Poached Pears Stuffed with Ricotta, Chocolate, Almonds and, *36, 37*–38
and Peach Cobbler, 181
Pear, and Chocolate Bread Pudding, 44–45
Pistachio, and Almond Bark, 136–37
Sautéed, Chocolate Bread with, 166–67
selecting and storing, 12
Sorbet for Dum-Dums with Almond Ding, 162–63
Chocolate:
    Bittersweet, Mousse, Pear and Fig Chutney with, *120,* 121
    bitter vs. bittersweet, 3
    Bread with Sautéed Cherries, 166–67
    Brownies with Dried Cherries, 134–35
    Cassis Truffles, 217–18, *219*
    Cherry Biscotti, Peppery, 138–39
    Cherry Fruitcake, *127,* 132–33
    and Fresh Candied Cherry Cake with Roasted Almond Crème Anglaise, *168,* 169–70
    Frozen Caramel Mousse with Sherry-Glazed Pears, Salted Almonds and, 39–40, *41*
    Hazelnut, and Apricot Dacquoise with Apricot Sauce, *144,* 145–46
    Marsala-Poached Pears Stuffed with Ricotta, Almonds, Cherries and, *36, 37*–38
    melting, 3
    Mocha Icing, 74
    Pear, and Cherry Bread Pudding, 44–45
    Pistachio, Almond, and Cherry Bark, 136–37
    Prune, Coffee, and Amaretto Tiramisù, 128–29
    Rum Glaze, 54
    Sauce, Anise-Orange Ice Cream Profiteroles with, 90–93, *91*
    Soufflé Cake with Prunes, Cranberries, and Kumquats in Port, 118–19
    Tangerine Sorbet, 97
    White, Sauce, Free-Style Lemon Tartlets with, 105–6, *107*

Chopping, 7

Chutney, Pear and Fig, with Bittersweet
    Chocolate Mousse, *120,* 121

Cider:
    Buckwheat Cake with Apples Poached in,
        21–22, *23*
    Sabayon, Spiced Apple Charlotte with, 28–29

Citrus fruits, 61–115
    selecting and storing, 12
    see also specific citrus fruits

Cobblers:
    Cherry Almond, 164–65
    Mango-Blackberry Almond, 165
    Mixed-Berry Almond, 165
    Nectarine and Blueberry, with Big Fluffy
        Biscuits, 180–81
    Peach and Berry or Cherry, with Big Fluffy
        Biscuits, 181

Cocoa powder, 3

Coconut:
    Cranzac Cookies, 147
    Flatties, Mango Napoleons with Lime
        Custard and, 58–61, *59*
    Glaze, Papaya Cake with, 53–54
    Pineapple Cookies, 65
    Pineapple Flan, 70
    Rum "Kaya," Lime Cream Puffs with
        Sugared Almonds and, 102–3
    Toasted, Kiwi, and Pineapple Baked Hawaii,
        55–57

Coffee:
    -Caramelized Bananas, Butterscotch
        Pudding with, 71–73, *72*
    Crunchies, Banana Cake with Mocha Icing
        and, 74–75
    Prune, Chocolate, and Amaretto Tiramisù,
        128–29

Compotes and poached fruits:
    Apples Poached in Cider, 21–22, *23*
    Bananas, Coffee-Caramelized, 71, *72,* 73
    Berries Romanoff with Iced Sour Cream, 202
    Blackberries in Port, 119
    Cherries, Sautéed, 166–67
    Melon with Three Flavored Syrups, 155–57,
        156

Orange-Honey Fruit Salad with Bostock,
    80, 81–82
Peaches in Red Wine, 171
Peaches Poached in Wine Syrup, 176, *177*
Pear and Fig Chutney, *120,* 121
Pears, Honey-Poached, 34–35
Pears, Marsala-Poached, Stuffed with
    Ricotta, Chocolate, Almonds, and
    Cherries, *36,* 37–38
Pears, Saffron-Poached, 46–47
Pears, Sherry-Glazed, *39,* 40–41
Pears, Spice-Baked, 42–43
Plum and Berry, 189
Prunes, Cranberries, and Kumquats in Port,
    118–19
Quinces, Poached, 31
Strawberries, Sugared, in Red Wine, 194–95

Concord Sorbet, 154

Confections. *See* Candies and confections

Cookies:
    Coconut Flatties, 58–60, *59*
    Cranzac, 147
    Lemon Quaresimali, 110–11
    Peanut, Crispy, 101
    Peppery Chocolate-Cherry Biscotti, 138–39
    Pineapple Coconut, 65
    Rosemary, Tomato Jam with, 220–21

Cookware:
    heavy-gauge vs. flimsy, 5
    nonreactive, 8
    saucepans, 8
    skillets, 9

Cornmeal:
    Polenta Cake with Saffron-Poached Pears,
        46–47
    Polenta Topping, Apple and Pear Crisp
        with Grappa-Soaked Raisins and, 20
    Shortcakes with Spice-Baked Pears,
        42–43

Cranberry(ies):
    and Apple Crisp, 19
    Chocolate Soufflé Cake with Prunes,
        Kumquats and, in Port, 118–19
    Cornmeal Shortcakes with Spice-Baked
        Pears and, 43

Cranzac Cookies, 147
Upside-Down Gingerbread, 183
Cranzac Cookies, 147
Creaming, 7
Cream Puffs, Lime, with Sugared Almonds
and Coconut-Rum "Kaya," 102–3
Crème Anglaise, Roasted Almond, *168,*
169–70
Crème Brûlée, Lemon-Ginger, 108–9
Crêpes, Buckwheat, with Tangerine
Butterscotch Sauce, 94–95
Crisps:
Apple, Gravenstein, and Blackberry, 18–19
Apple and Cranberry, 19
Apple and Mince, 19
Apple and Pear, with Polenta Topping and
Grappa-Soaked Raisins, 20
Berry and Amaretti, 173
Peach and Amaretti, 172–73
Custard:
Blackberry and Lemon Gratin, 208–9
Caramelized Pineapple Flan, *68,* 69–70
Lemon-Ginger Crème Brûlée, 108–9
Lime, Mango Napoleons with Coconut
Flatties and, 58–61, *59*
Pineapple Coconut Flan, 70

Dacquoise, Hazelnut, Apricot, and Chocolate,
with Apricot Sauce, *144,* 145–46
Date:
Brazil Nut, and Ginger Tart, 122–23
Ginger, and Candied Pineapple Fruitcake,
125–26, *127*
Nut Torte, Syrian-Style, 124
Ding, Almond, 162–63
Dried fruit, 118–47
selecting and storing, 12
see also specific dried fruits

Egg(s):
at room temperature, 8
whites, whipping, 4
see also Meringue(s)

Fig(s):
Fresh, and Raspberry Tart with Honey, 150–51
Fresh, Homemade Ricotta with Chestnut
Honey and, 152
and Pear Chutney with Bittersweet
Chocolate Mousse, *120, 121*
Filo Triangles, Apricot, with Retsina Syrup, 142–43
Financiers:
Blackberry, *206,* 207
Peach, Plum, or Nectarine, 207
Flan:
Caramelized Pineapple, *68,* 69–70
Pineapple Coconut, 70
Flour, measuring, 4
Folding, 7
Formaggio, Honeyed Strawberries *al,* 199
Frangipane Tart, Pineapple, 66–67
Freezing desserts, 6
Frozen desserts:
Kiwi, Pineapple, and Toasted Coconut
Baked Hawaii, 55–57
Pomegranate Granita, 159
Riesling Sabayon, 83
see also Ice cream; Sorbet(s)
Fruitcakes:
Chocolate Cherry, *127,* 132–33
Date, Ginger, and Candied Pineapple,
125–26, *127*
Fruits:
selecting and storing, 10–15
washing, 5
Fruit Salad, Orange-Honey, with Bostock,
80, 81–82

Gâteau Basque, Prune, 130–31
Gelatin-based desserts:
Panna Cotta with Blueberries, Ranch, 210–11
Strawberry Bavarian with Orange-Rhubarb
Sauce, 200–201
Tangerine Juice, Jellied, 96
Ginger:
Brazil Nut, and Date Tart, 122–23
Date, and Candied Pineapple Fruitcake,
125–26, *127*

Ginger *(cont.)*:
Gingery Lemonade, 115
Lemon Crème Brûlée, 108–9
-and-Sake Syrup, 155–57, *156*
Gingerbread, upside-down:
Cranberry, Pear, Orange, Plum, or Pluot, 183
Nectarine and Raspberry, 182–83
Glazes:
Brown Sugar, 86–87
Chocolate-Rum, 54
Coconut, 53–54
Pineapple, 66–67
Toffee, 185
Graham Cracker Crust, 98–99, 214
Granita, Pomegranate, 159
Grapefruit, 12
Pink, Champagne Sorbet, 104
Grape Sorbets, Wine, Duo of, 154
Grappa-Soaked Raisins, Apple and Pear Crisp
with Polenta Topping and, 20
Gratin, Blackberry and Lemon, 208–9
Greasing pans, 5

Hazelnut(s):
Apricot, and Chocolate Dacquoise with
Apricot Sauce, *144,* 145–46
Lemon Quaresimali, 110–11
Honey(ed):
Orange Fruit Salad with Bostock, *80,* 81–82
-Poached Pears, Stilton Shortcakes with
Candied Pecans and, 34–35
Retsina Syrup, 142–43
Strawberries *al Formaggio,* 199

Ice cream:
Anise-Orange, Profiteroles with Chocolate
Sauce, 90–93, *91*
Apricot, *Tartufi,* 140–41
Toasted Coconut, 55–56
Icings, Mocha, 74
Ingredients:
gathering before starting to assemble, 4
quality of, 5

Jam, Tomato, 220–21
Jellied Tangerine Juice, 96
Jelly, Peanut, and Butter Linzertorte, 153

"Kaya," Coconut-Rum, Lime Cream Puffs
with Sugared Almonds and, 102–3
Kirsch Syrup, 174
Kiwi fruit, 13
Pineapple, and Toasted Coconut Baked
Hawaii, 55–57
Kumquats, Chocolate Soufflé Cake with
Prunes, Cranberries and, in Port, 118–19

Lemon(s):
and Blackberry Gratin, 208–9
Ginger Crème Brûlée, 108–9
Meyer, selecting and storing, 12
Quaresimali, 110–11
Quick-Candied, 114
Superlemon Soufflé, 112–13
Tartlets, Free-Style, with White Chocolate
Sauce, 105–6, *107*
Lemonade, Gingery, 115
Lilikoi. *See* Passion fruit
Lime:
Champagne Syrup, 155–57, *156*
Cream Puffs with Sugared Almonds and
Coconut-Rum "Kaya," 102–3
Custard, Mango Napoleons with Coconut
Flatties and, 58–61, *59*
Margarita Sorbet with Crispy Peanut
Cookies, 101
Marshmallow Pie, 98–100
Linzertorte, Peanut, Butter, and Jelly, 153

Manchego Cheese, Quince Marmalade with,
32, 33
Mango(es):
Blackberry Almond Cobbler, 165
and Lilikoi Butter, 76–77
Napoleons with Lime Custard and Coconut
Flatties, 58–60, *59*

peeling and cutting, 63

selecting and storing, 13

Tarte Tatin with Crushed Blackberries, *62,* 63-64

Maple-Walnut Sauce, 24, 27

Margarita Sorbet with Crispy Peanut Cookies, 101

Marmalade, Quince, with Manchego Cheese, *32,* 33

Marsala-Poached Pears Stuffed with Ricotta, Chocolate, Almonds, and Cherries, *36,* 37-38

Marshmallow Lime Pie, 98-100

Marzipan and Apricot Tart, 178-79

Mascarpone:

Cheesecake with Mixed Berries, 214-15

Homemade, 216

Prune, Coffee, Chocolate, and Amaretto Tiramisù, 128-29

Measuring:

flour, 4

scales and, 4

Measuring cups, 4

Melon:

with Three Flavored Syrups, 155-57, *156*

Watermelon and Sake Sorbet, 158

Meringue(s):

Almond, Baskets, Strawberries in Red Wine Syrup with, *196,* 197-98

Blood Orange Sorbet Surprise, 84-85

Free-Style Lemon Tartlets with White Chocolate Sauce, 105-6, *107*

Hazelnut, Apricot, and Chocolate Dacquoise with Apricot Sauce, *144,* 145-46

Mince and Apple Crisp, 19

Mint-Chartreuse Syrup, 155-57, *156*

Mise en place, 4

Mocha Icing, 74-75

Mousse:

Bittersweet Chocolate, Pear and Fig Chutney with, *120,* 121

Frozen Caramel, with Sherry-Glazed Pears, Chocolate, and Salted Almonds, 39-40, *41*

Muscat Sorbet, 154

Napoleons, Mango, with Lime Custard and Coconut Flatties, 58-61, *59*

Nectarine(s):

and Blueberry Cobbler with Big Fluffy Biscuits, 180-81

Financiers, 207

Plum, and Blackberry Charlotte, 186-87

and Raspberry Upside-Down Gingerbread, 182-83

in Red Wine, 171

selecting and storing, 14

Nonreactive cookware, 8

Nut(s):

Date Torte, Syrian-Style, 124

pulverizing, 8

toasting, 9

see also specific nuts

Oats, in Cranzac Cookies, 147

Orange(s):

Allspice Cake, with Brown Sugar Glaze, 86-87

Anise Ice Cream Profiteroles with Chocolate Sauce, 90-93, *91*

Blood, Sorbet Surprise, 84-85

Blood, Soup with Frozen Riesling Sabayon, 83

Candied, Ricotta Cake with Rosy Rhubarb Sauce and, 88-89

Honey Fruit Salad with Bostock, *80,* 81-82

Rhubarb Sauce, Strawberry Bavarian with, 200-201

selecting and storing, 12

Upside-Down Gingerbread, 183

Panna Cotta with Blueberries, Ranch, 210-11

Pans, greasing for baking, 5

Papaya(s), 13

Cake with Coconut Glaze, 53-54

Passion fruit (lilikoi), 13

juicing, 77

and Mango Butter, 76-77

Pastries:
    Anise-Orange Ice Cream Profiteroles
       with Chocolate Sauce, 90–93, *91*
    Apricot Filo Triangles with Retsina Syrup,
       142–43
    Boysenberry Turnovers, 203–4, *205*
    Lime Cream Puffs with Sugared Almonds
       and Coconut-Rum "Kaya," 102–3
    see also Pie(s); Tarts
Pastry Cream Gâteau Basque, 130–31
Peach(es):
    and Amaretti Crisp, 172–73
    and Berry or Cherry Cobbler, 181
    Financiers, 207
    Poached in Wine Syrup, 176, *177*
    in Red Wine, 171
    selecting and storing, 14
    Semifreddo, 174–75
Peanut:
    Butter, and Jelly Linzertorte, 153
    Cookies, Crispy, Margarita Sorbet with, 101
Pear(s):
    and Apple Crisp with Polenta Topping and
       Grappa-Soaked Raisins, 20
    Cherry, and Chocolate Bread Pudding, 44–45
    and Fig Chutney with Bittersweet Chocolate
       Mousse, *120,* 121
    Honey-Poached, Stilton Shortcakes with
       Candied Pecans and, 34–35
    Marsala-Poached, Stuffed with Ricotta,
       Chocolate, Almonds, and Cherries,
       36, 37–38
    Saffron-Poached, Polenta Cake with, 46–47
    selecting and storing, 14
    Sherry-Glazed, Frozen Caramel Mousse
       with Chocolate, Salted Almonds and,
       39–40, *41*
    Spice-Baked, Cornmeal Shortcakes with,
       42–43
    Upside-Down Gingerbread, 183
Pecans:
    Candied, Stilton Shortcakes with Honey-
       Poached Pears and, 34–35
    Gravenstein Apple and Blackberry Crisp,
       18–19

Peppery Chocolate-Cherry Biscotti, 138–39
Pie(s):
    Crust, Graham Cracker, 98–99, 214
    Lime Marshmallow, 98–100
    Mixed Berry, 212–13
Pineapple:
    Candied, Date, and Ginger Fruitcake,
       125–26, *127*
    Caramelized, Flan, *68,* 69–70
    Coconut Cookies, 65
    Coconut Flan, 70
    Frangipane Tart, 66–67
    Kiwi, and Toasted Coconut Baked Hawaii,
       55–57
    and Mango Napoleons with Lime Custard
       and Coconut Flatties, 58–61, *59*
    selecting and storing, 14
Pistachio, Almond, and Cherry Bark, 136–37
Plum(s):
    Financiers, 207
    Marzipan Tart, 179
    Nectarine, and Blackberry Charlotte,
       186–87
    selecting and storing, 15
    Streusel Cake, Spiced, with Toffee Glaze,
       184–85
    Tart, Yeasted, with Red Wine–Plum Sauce,
       191
    Three-Seed Shortcakes with Red Berries
       and, *188,* 189–90
    Upside-Down Gingerbread, 183
Pluot Upside-Down Gingerbread, 183
Poached fruits. *See* Compotes and poached
    fruits
Polenta:
    Cake with Saffron-Poached Pears, 46–47
    Topping, Apple and Pear Crisp with Grappa-
       Soaked Raisins and, 20
Pomegranate Granita, 159
Port:
    Blackberries in, 119
    Chocolate Soufflé Cake with Prunes,
       Cranberries, and Kumquats in, 118–19
Profiteroles, Anise-Orange Ice Cream, with
       Chocolate Sauce, 90–93, *91*

Prune(s), 12
    Chocolate Soufflé Cake with Cranberries,
        Kumquats and, in Port, 118-19
    Coffee, Chocolate, and Amaretto Tiramisù,
        128-29
    Gâteau Basque, 130-31
Puddings:
    Bread, Pear, Cherry, and Chocolate, 44-45
    Butterscotch, with Coffee-Caramelized
        Bananas, 71-73, 72
    see also Custard; Gelatin-based desserts;
        Mousse
Puff Pastry, Whole-Wheat Express, Apple
    Tart with, and Maple-Walnut Sauce,
    24-27
Pulverizing, 8

Quaresimali, Lemon, 110-11
Quince:
    and Apple Tarte Tatin, 30-31
    Marmalade with Manchego Cheese, 32, 33
    poaching, 31
    selecting and storing, 15

Raisins, Grappa-Soaked, Apple and Pear Crisp
    with Polenta Topping and, 20
Raspberry(ies):
    Apricot Marzipan Tart, 179
    and Fresh Fig Tart with Honey, 150-51
    and Nectarine Upside-Down Gingerbread,
        182-83
    and Peach Cobbler, 181
    Red Wine–Plum Sauce, Yeasted Plum Tart
        with, 191
    and Rhubarb Tart with Almond Nougatine,
        48-49
    selecting and storing, 11
    Three-Seed Shortcakes with Plums and
        Red Berries, 188, 189-90
    see also Berry(ies)
Reducing, 8
Retsina Syrup, Apricot Filo Triangles with,
    142-43

Rhubarb:
    Orange Sauce, Strawberry Bavarian with,
        200-201
    and Raspberry Tart, 49
    Sauce, Rosy, Ricotta Cake with Candied
        Orange and, 88-89
    selecting and storing, 15
    Tart with Almond Nougatine, 48-49
Ricotta:
    Cake with Candied Orange and Rosy
        Rhubarb Sauce, 88-89
    Homemade, with Fresh Figs and Chestnut
        Honey, 152
    Marsala-Poached Pears Stuffed with
        Chocolate, Almonds, Cherries and, 36,
        37-38
Riesling Sabayon, Frozen, Blood Orange Soup
    with, 83
Room temperature, ingredients brought to, 8
Rose Geranium and Blackberry Gratin, 209
Rosemary Cookies, Tomato Jam with, 220-21
Rum:
    Caramel, 58, 59, 60
    Chocolate Glaze, 54
    Coconut "Kaya," Lime Cream Puffs with
        Sugared Almonds and, 102-3

Sabayon:
    Cider, Spiced Apple Charlotte with, 28-29
    Riesling, Frozen, Blood Orange Soup with,
        83
Saffron-Poached Pears, Polenta Cake with,
    46-47
Sake:
    -and-Ginger Syrup, 155-57, 156
    and Watermelon Sorbet, 158
Salad, Orange-Honey Fruit, with Bostock,
    80, 81-82
Salt, coarse, 5
Saucepans, 8
Sauces:
    Apple, 44-45
    Apricot, 140-41, 145-46
    Chocolate, 90, 91, 93

Sauces (cont.):
    Cider Sabayon, 28-29
    Mango and Lilikoi Butter, 76-77
    Maple-Walnut, 24, 27
    Orange-Rhubarb, 200
    Red Wine-Plum, 191
    Rhubarb, Rosy, 88-89
    Roasted Almond Crème Anglaise, *168*, 169-70
    Rum Caramel, 58, *59*, 60
    Tangerine Butterscotch, 94-95
    White Chocolate, 105-6
    see also Glazes; Syrups
Scales, 4
Seed, Three-, Shortcakes with Plums and
    Red Berries, *188*, 189-90
Semifreddo, Peach, 174-75
Sherry-Glazed Pears, Frozen Caramel Mousse
    with Chocolate, Salted Almonds and,
    39-40, *41*
Shortbread, Rosemary, Tomato Jam with,
    220-21
Shortcakes:
    Cornmeal, with Spice-Baked Pears, 42-43
    Stilton, with Candied Pecans and Honey-
    Poached Pears, 34-35
    Three-Seed, with Plums and Red Berries,
    188, 189-90
Simmering, 9
Skillets, 9
Sorbet(s):
    Blood Orange, Surprise, 84-85
    Cherry, for Dum-Dums with Almond Ding,
    162-63
    Chocolate-Tangerine, 97
    Kiwi, 55
    Margarita, with Crispy Peanut Cookies, 101
    Pineapple, 55
    Pink Grapefruit Champagne, 104
    Watermelon and Sake, 158
    Wine Grape, Duo of, 154
Soufflé(s):
    Chocolate, Cake with Prunes, Cranberries,
    and Kumquats in Port, 118-19
    Superlemon, 112-13
Soup, Blood Orange, with Frozen Riesling
    Sabayon, 83

Sour Cream, Iced, Berries Romanoff with, 202
Spice(d):
    Apple Charlotte with Cider Sabayon,
    28-29
    -Baked Pears, Cornmeal Shortcakes with,
    42-43
    Plum Streusel Cake with Toffee Glaze,
    184-85
Sponge Cake, 128
    Peach Semifreddo, 174-75
Stilton Shortcakes with Candied Pecans
    and Honey-Poached Pears, 34-35
Stirring, 9
Strawberry(ies):
    Bavarian with Orange-Rhubarb Sauce,
    200-201
    Honeyed, *al Formaggio,* 199
    in Red Wine Syrup with Almond Meringue
    Baskets, *196,* 197-98
    selecting and storing, 15
    Sugared, in Red Wine, Caramelized Brioche
    with, 194-95
    Three-Seed Shortcakes with Plums and
    Red Berries, *188,* 189-90
    see also Berry(ies)
Streusel Cake, Spiced Plum, with Toffee Glaze,
    184-85
Superlemon Soufflé, 112-13
Syrian-Style Date-Nut Torte, 124
Syrups:
    Champagne-Lime, 155-57, *156*
    Chartreuse-Mint, 155-57, *156*
    Coffee-Amaretto, 128-29
    Kirsch, 174
    Red Wine, Strawberries in, *196,* 197-98
    Retsina, 142-43
    Sake-and-Ginger, 155-57, *156*
    Wine, Peaches Poached in, 176, *177*

Tangerine(s):
    Butterscotch Sauce, Buckwheat Crêpes
    with, 94-95
    Chocolate Sorbet, 97
    Juice, Jellied, 96
    selecting and storing, 12

Tarts:
    Apple, with Whole-Wheat Express
        Puff Pastry and Maple-Walnut Sauce,
        24-27
    Apple and Quince Tarte Tatin, 30-31
    Apricot and Marzipan, 178-79
    Brazil Nut, Date, and Ginger, 122-23
    Fig and Raspberry, with Honey, 150-51
    Lemon Tartlets, Free-Style, with White
        Chocolate Sauce, 105-6, *107*
    Mango Tarte Tatin with Crushed
        Blackberries, *62,* 63-64
    Pineapple Frangipane, 66-67
    Plum Marzipan Tart, 179
    Prune Gâteau Basque, 130-31
    Raspberry- or Blackberry-Apricot Marzipan
        Tart, 179
    Rhubarb, with Almond Nougatine, 48-49
    Rhubarb and Raspberry, 49
    Yeasted Plum, with Red Wine–Plum Sauce,
        191
Tartufi, Apricot Ice Cream, 140-41
Thermometers, 4
Three-Seed Shortcakes with Plums and
    Red Berries, *188,* 189-90
Tiramisù, Prune, Coffee, Chocolate, and
    Amaretto, 128-29
Toasting nuts, 9
Toffee Glaze, Spiced Plum Streusel Cake with,
    184-85
Tomato Jam with Rosemary Cookies, 220-21
Tortes:
    Date-Nut, Syrian-Style, 124
    Peanut, Butter, and Jelly Linzertorte,
        153
Tropical fruits, 53-77
    see also specific tropical fruits
Truffles, Cassis, 217-18, *219*
Turnovers, Boysenberry, 203-4, *205*

Walnut(s):
    Date-Nut Torte, Syrian-Style, 124
    Gravenstein Apple and Blackberry Crisp, 18-19
    Maple Sauce, 24, 27
Watermelon and Sake Sorbet, 158
Whipped Cream, 35
Whipping, 9
    egg whites, 4
Whisking, 9
White Chocolate Sauce, Free-Style Lemon
    Tartlets with, 105-6, *107*
Whole-Wheat Express Puff Pastry, Apple Tart
    with, and Maple-Walnut Sauce, 24-27
Wine:
    Champagne-Lime Syrup, 155-57, *156*
    Champagne Pink Grapefruit Sorbet, 104
    Grape Sorbets, Duo of, 154
    Marsala-Poached Pears Stuffed with
        Ricotta, Chocolate, Almonds, and
        Cherries, *36,* 37-38
    Port, Blackberries in, 119
    Port, Chocolate Soufflé Cake with Prunes,
        Cranberries, and Kumquats in, 118-19
    Red, Caramelized Brioche with Sugared
        Strawberries in, 194-95
    Red, Peaches in, 171
    Red, Plum Sauce, Yeasted Plum Tart with, 191
    Red, Syrup, Strawberries in, with Almond
        Meringue Baskets, *196,* 197-98
    Riesling Sabayon, Frozen, Blood Orange
        Soup with, 83
    Sherry-Glazed Pears, Frozen Caramel
        Mousse with Chocolate, Salted Almonds
        and, 39-40, *41*
    Syrup, Peaches Poached in, 176, *177*

Yeasted Plum Tart with Red Wine–Plum Sauce,
    191